THE GOOD, THE BAD, AND THE BLESSED

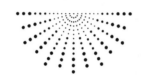

THE GOOD, THE BAD, AND THE BLESSED

A STORY OF EVERYONE WHO IS AS LUCKY AS ME

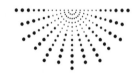

MARC THROOP

For my wife Peg,

my family,

and those who have mentored me.

CONTENTS

PREFACE

I should have died; could have and wonder why I didn't.

What I've done in my life made me question whether the answer was as easy for others to understand as it is for me now. Not until my thirties did I get that answer. In fact, a lot of things became clearer. Not easier, but *clearer*.

Guarding our hearts is perhaps the most complex and challenging journey we will ever take during our time on earth if we genuinely desire to see good—and be good—in all situations. Notice I say "desire," as it is impossible to accomplish seeing and being good in every little thing we do.

When we're young, we feel physically immortal. As a result, we make some extremely dumb decisions along the way. We have expectations for ourselves and our lives, and some of them are unrealistic. Time and time again, we're bombarded by things that cause guilt, self-blame, regret, and other negative emotions inside our hearts and minds that are not only unhealthy but have us struggling to remove those feelings from our lives.

On the other side of the coin are those very same feelings we want others to experience when they've offended or hurt us, causing us to fall into one of the most vile and complicated feelings there is:

hate. On top of that, we find we can't go back and change those feelings or any of the crazy decisions we—or anyone else—have made.

The good news? None of us has to feel condemnation from any decision we've ever made or feeling we've experienced! There is only one person who was perfect, and I'm sure that it's not you, and I'm absolutely, 100% sure it's not me.

Through the experiences any of us go through, we can live free and genuinely see the good in everything. I've learned this through my journey. However, it is easier said than done.

I certainly hope that the following thoughts and experiences I've endured provide a way to help overcome and relieve any feelings of self-condemnation for anyone reading this. We may be guilty of making poor decisions, but freedom from regrettable times can be provided and accepted with open arms.

You may never forget your guilt. You may not even forget the horrible things done to you... but you do *not* have to let them define you. Some people may try to remind you of your mistakes. It's difficult not to believe them sometimes, but there *is* a way out.

-Marc Throop

1

THE BEGINNING

For the most part, I was a pretty decent guy. But every once in a while, I did some stupid things.

When someone asks where I came from and how my childhood was, I admit I was in the "fortunate" camp. Having grown up in the little town of Romeo, Michigan, I had the pleasure of truly experiencing small-town life. Romeo is about a half-hour north of Detroit, and even though the big city was reasonably close, rarely did I go there. For some reason, it seemed like a day's journey.

Stores lined Romeo's Main Street, and almost everyone did their business in town. You could go for a walk at 10:00 on a Friday night by yourself and feel safe. It has changed a great deal since then, but it still possesses the small-town feel that many people today desire.

The work ethic in the late 1950s and '60s had to be tremendous to survive. Technology has made life so much simpler, and the development of machines, tools, and other modern marvels allows us to even make work easier. "We're having leftovers tonight, so just throw them in the microwave!" wasn't a phrase you'd often hear. Just imagine today's kids having to make popcorn on the stove. We didn't have popcorn poppers, much less the ability to microwave a bag.

All the processes of preparing and cooking food, building anything, or even watching something weren't nearly as effortless as they are now. Looking back at the way it was done is more than nostalgic. We never imagined machines that would make a great cup of coffee or heat a meal in seconds.

My parents lived in a small apartment in town when they were first married, but my father and grandfather quickly got busy building the home my siblings and I grew up in. Yes, they mixed cement, pounded nails, and everything else that made that house. They had no contractor, no work crew of ten or more people, and no big machines to build it.

It was a little home with three small bedrooms, a kitchen, living room, an unfinished basement, and a garage. Our house only had one bathroom, which was tiny and had to accommodate all five of us. Mom, Dad, my sister, brother, and I often fought over it. Keep in mind that we're a very tall family, so space was at a premium.

The great thing is that we felt as though we had a wonderful house, and that was because my parents made it a home and not just a house. That place is still in our family; my nephew lives there. I haven't been back to Romeo or that house in several years, but it'll always be my natural home. The memories that came out of living with my family—all the holidays, games, and countless times of walking through the front door and having that feeling of "Now I'm home"—are irreplaceable. I could walk through that door today and feel the same way.

Our backyard was fantastic! It was big enough to play neighborhood sandlot baseball, football, and kickball games. There are several distinct memories of that yard I don't think I'll ever forget...

Several of us were playing baseball one day. David Shanlian—a neighbor—swung the bat, but unfortunately, Jeff Lahde, another neighbor boy, walked into the path of the swing and was struck directly in the head. It was a horrific sight, and we were stunned, not only from having viewed the accident but seeing blood pour from Jeff's head. To this day, I can't understand how he survived that blow.

Probably the worst thing for Jeff was that he had to sit out a few days before he could play again. Concussion? More than likely, but we never heard that word back then or knew the severity of what it could cause. Instead, we treated such injuries as glitches in our playtime.

Was it dangerous in that backyard for me? Nah. Nothing could hurt me, not even when I jumped off the roof of our house. Despite it being about twenty feet in the air, amazingly, I didn't die. And the time I lost control of my bicycle and careened head-first into a tree? Well, I was knocked out, but I didn't die that time either.

Remember, we think we're immortal at that age. No fear!

I also remember playing football with my friends in our backyard, and suddenly, we glanced up and saw an enormous sphere racing through the sky. It looked like it was on fire and left a smoke trail that stayed in the sky for what seemed like forever. The nightly news—which only lasted a half-hour, thank goodness—reported that it was a meteor, and it wound up falling into the Detroit River. We thought that information was the biggest story in the country! What a crazy experience.

We were careful, too. The man living next door had a reputation of being mean and dangerous, but even worse than him was his cat, which we were told had eaten Mr. Whitsey's arm. I recall sometimes seeing a cat the size of a house, and I always ran back into our home for safety. The dual-threat also meant we kept a spotter in case we kicked a field goal too long or hit a baseball too far. We made sure that cat wasn't going to eat our arms while a runner chased down the stray ball and retrieved it from the neighbor's yard.

I don't remember the last time we played in our backyard, and that's a bizarre thing to think about. Playing basketball in the driveway, riding bikes with the neighborhood kids, and other experiences never dawn on you when they're occurring that they won't ever happen again. When you're young, it seems as if there are no "last times."

Christmas was always special when we were little kids, but it was also our most celebrated time of year when my siblings and I had families of our own. We still went back to Mom and Dad's and had Christmas. Such is one of the significant impacts of having a family, especially as parents, that means everything.

There are also certain Christmas presents you get over the years that you remember more than others, and one of mine was a kind of miniature pinball machine. That thing got played with so much on Christmas day that I don't think it ever got a rest from having everyone take their turn with it. We all heard a loud sound early the next morning as my dad got up for work. Lo and behold, he'd stepped right in the middle of that little pinball machine and completely shattered it.

If there were events in my life at that early stage that someone wanted to label as "forever scarring," that would have been one— such a terrible experience for an eight-year-old! I thought nothing would ever be as bad as that. Of course, I was wrong.

2

READY TO GROW

Wh

hen it was time that I realized my dream of attending school was finally coming true after many years, my destination was North Grade School. Can you guess the name of the other elementary? Yep, it was South Grade School.

Conveniently, North Grade School was only one block away from our house, which meant I could walk to school, walk home for lunch, and then go back to school for the afternoon. Sadly, our society has turned into one where you probably can't trust your kids will be safe walking to and from school in many areas.

The school's ambiance was exciting and eye-opening, and the building was a magical place in the center of our neighborhood. The best part of that building was probably the obstacles that wouldn't let our imaginations rest, as we wondered just how exciting getting to fully experience them might be.

Long, tubular fire escape chutes that started on the third floor and went all the way to the ground were things that made us hope for a fire drill—or even a fire—because that meant we'd get to go down them. Whenever there was a fire drill, the teacher opened the door to the third-floor classroom, and most boys and girls knew their chute fantasies were about to come true. Sliding down that metal beast and then coming to rest on the ground below was a rush of joy for most kids, but some were terrified of going down.

The problem was that only those in the fifth and sixth grades could slide down them, since their classrooms were on the third floor. The rest of the poor saps on floors one and two had to evacuate down the boring stairs and watch in envy as the third-floor champions slid down the fire escapes. We almost wanted to bow down to them for their bravery. It was just another reason to make sure we didn't get into too much trouble and do well enough academically to escalate to the top floor.

Ahh... the elementary years, where everything was innocent and uncomplicated. Reminiscing back to those years, I look at them now and think about what life was for kids then and how easy it seemed. However, going through it wasn't all fun and games.

Speaking of games, one of the most thrilling experiences available to us was recess and the opportunity to play softball on the playground—innocent mostly, but the real excitement came when the school bus made one of its lunch runs. We had a pitcher that timed it just right so that we could take aim at the big yellow limousine from home plate as it drove by the homerun fence. I don't remember ever hitting it, but the effort was solid and even included a few homers in the big "recess softball game."

Hitting those buses? Not a wise thing to do, but it was an early life experience where one terrible decision was just the start of making many more in my life. Hey, don't judge! Everyone reading this has made bad decisions, as that's what happens in the lives of all men and women.

My younger years were also a time in America that was delicate, even though I didn't realize it. Being an eight-year-old elementary school student, I can't say I spent much time worrying about the world. But, there are things that I *do* recall about that era...

President John F. Kennedy, Jr. was shot in 1963, and I was on the school playground when I heard the awful news.

Back then, there were three channels on the television— CBS, NBC, and ABC—and we also got Channel 9, but it was hardly ever watched. On an excellent night, we could pick up Channel 50 out of Canada, but most of the time, it was grainy and unwatchable. When the TV was on at night, we mostly put it on whatever channel we wanted and never changed it since there was no remote control. Can you imagine kids tolerating that kind of abuse today?

Even though we only had only a few television stations, the JFK assassination news coverage lasted for days, and it was the only thing on every one of those channels. No cartoons, soap operas, game shows, or anything else, and that was understandable. There was constant coverage of what was happening with the assassination, JFK's funeral, Lee Harvey Oswald's shooting, and anything else that had to do with the case.

The event that broke the non-stop coverage was the Sunday National Football League games. People were finally trying to get back to some sense of normalcy, even though it was almost impossible due to that tragic historical event. Still, the NFL games gave them something else to focus on, if only for a few hours once a week.

Martin Luther King, Jr. and Robert Kennedy were also assassinated in the '60s, and those horrific events captured the divide America was experiencing. Three people of such huge historical importance were gunned down in a matter of five years, with all three having quite a bit of popularity, even though some people didn't necessarily agree with all the political stances the others were taking. When it came down to it, they were all good people.

The death of Dr. King struck a chord with the Black communities, as the Civil Rights Movement of the 1960s was in full swing and doing a phenomenal job at shedding light on the current and past regretful circumstances in America. In addition to the assassinations, the Vietnam War was going on, the age of Aquarius with the Flower Children—or hippies, as they were called—was moving, and the beginning of what I considered real music was unfolding.

Growing up during that time, we saw the start of Rock and Roll, the introduction of the Beatles in America, and countless bands flooding the music scene. One of my earliest memories is watching the Beatles on *The Ed Sullivan Show*. My brother had a cheap voice recorder and tried to tape that segment. It was such a terrible device; we barely heard the Beatles, but there were plenty of screeches and static. It didn't matter. We had a piece of the greatest music fad that's ever surged through America.

Long hair on men was famous then, but the older generation made fun of them and called them some pretty interesting names. Fighting the battle of whether their sons could grow out their hair was no doubt one struggle some parents had.

Robby Lahde, Mark House, and I let our hair grow out a bit, but nothing too extreme since our parents wouldn't let it happen. When we were in the seventh grade, the three of us decided we would go to the barber and shave our heads, which was out of the norm back then. Ed Trim—how's that name for a barber's name?—was surprised when we told him what we wanted. When I got mine cut, there was so much grease built up in my scalp that I had to rush home to get it washed. Gross!

Afterward, we went down to Fred's Market, the local store that sold meat, bread, alcohol, and other things. We went there on many occasions to spend small amounts of money—always under a dollar —on a bag full of candy that grumpy old Fred let us get. Little did we know the bag of candy we picked out was probably worth a few bucks, but Fred always gave us the discount. I guess he wasn't so bad after all.

The best thing about getting our locks chopped off was that when the three of us walked in, Fred looked at us with the biggest smile. He was excited to see kids without hair rather than the long mops that were in style. He told us each to pick out a snack from the bakery section, and we thought we had hit the lottery!

At the time, that seemed like an incredible experience.

3

SMALL TOWN INDEPENDENCE

F red's Market was also where I always went to buy my
baseball cards, which happened a lot.

When my brother bought his cards, he always put a
Mickey Mantle card on his bike spokes to make a clicking noise
when he pedaled. He hated the Yankees, so it was a logical choice to
put their cards on his bike and make them look like trash within
twenty minutes. Boy, what a mistake that was—those cards are
worth thousands of dollars today.

Imagine a store three blocks from your house and walking there
unsupervised at ten years old today. It was normal for us.

One afternoon, there was a knock on my door, and it was a few
friends of mine. A knock on the door was how you got in touch with
your friends, a kind of modern-day texting back then.

They told me to get my bike, and we rode to a house up on
Hollister Street. We climbed a tree that was probably fifty feet tall.
Then we shimmied out onto a branch and rocked it until it snapped.
It came plummeting to the ground with us on it, and I bet we did
that half a dozen times.

A kid named Roger had one of the smaller branches stab him in the leg. We gaped in horror as the limb poked out of his skin and blood oozed from the wound. We just knew it was terrible. I can't remember who, but someone grabbed the branch and yanked it out. Someone asked, "Roger, are you okay?"

Crying like crazy, he nodded, and we went back to breaking branches. Eventually, Roger came back up and joined in again, bleeding and all.

There was a girl who was also with us, and she fell, hit her head, and was out like a light. We felt terrible because she was a girl. After a couple of minutes of being out, she came around and we told her she had to go home. You know, for health concerns. It had nothing to do with the fact that she was a girl. Hmm...

Amazingly, none of us died doing something as stupid as that.

In the sixth grade, I became the captain of the Safety Patrol, which meant I was the official "Big Man On Campus." I was tall, so that term would have been appropriate even if I hadn't garnered the role. People always looked at me differently because I was more vertically enhanced than the average bear. Those who remember *Yogi Bear* will understand that reference.

Remembering my height at different stages of my life is tough, but there are periods I do recall. When I was in kindergarten, I was five feet tall. In third grade, I was five feet, five inches tall. By the time I was in sixth grade, I was six feet tall! Then, I just kept growing.

As I entered the ninth grade, I became aware that I had always been taller than my teachers. Still, there was a guy named Stretch Lindburg (don't laugh). He was six feet, six inches tall, whereas I was only six feet, three inches tall. Incredibly, I grew four inches that year to an astounding six feet, seven inches, which made me taller than Stretch.

For all practical purposes, I grew up in the "White Picket Fence" family life. We didn't have much, but we had enough, and issues were never really talked about in terms of money. What I had compared to what my parents had as kids during the 1920s and 1930s was like living in luxury.

All three of Mom and Dad's kids graduated from college, with my sister graduating from Western Michigan University and my brother graduating from Northern Michigan University. My time in college was different from my siblings. I went to school on a full-ride basketball scholarship, which saved my parents a boatload of money. But again, our parents never talked to us about that "money thing" and discussed finances in general very little.

Mom and Dad were happy together and allowed us to grow up in the best of environments while providing us with whatever we needed and not necessarily what we wanted. I have a couple of distinct memories of my brother and sister as we grew up and tried our best to be good kids for our parents. Of course, that wasn't always the case. I was perhaps the one they had to watch out for the most, but seeing as how I'm the one writing this, I don't have to tell everything I was involved with. Besides, there's not enough room in this book.

Still, memories of my childhood with my siblings are far and few between due to our age difference. Judy is ten years older than me, and Rick is six years older. Of the three of us, I was the best looking and the smartest. Just ask me.

I recall a time when my sister was in college but home for the summer…

Judy was dating two guys at once, and one of them had a cool red convertible. He and Judy had gone out on a date, and when they came back, they decided to sit in his car in front of our house with the top down. I was playing down the street. Another vehicle turned the corner, and the guy in that car said something like, "Hey, Marc. Is your sister home?"

He was the other guy Judy was seeing! Never one to resist a little fun entertainment, I replied, "Sure she is. Go on down."

Billy Perry, Dudley Rashid, and I rode our bikes toward the house to see the interaction between the three of them that no doubt had to be uncomfortable, but especially for my guilty sister. Judy! What a heartbreaker. I don't think those guys came around much after that.

Fortunately, Judy married a guy named Tom Cvengros, and they've been together for the last fifty-plus years. Tom's a great guy. He's not my brother-in-law, but more like my brother. He's also a retired teacher and a big sports fan, so we talk a lot about those things when we're together. Judy and Tom have two children—Tom and Jill—and they're great kids. Even though they're over forty now, they're both still kids to me.

My brother, I think, was a little naughtier than my sister, but still a good kid. However, there was one situation that's probably the most memorable about him, and one I bet he'd like to forget!

Rick graduated from high school in 1969 and decided to attend Northern Michigan University in Marquette, Michigan, which was almost another country away from us. Like many people, we called the upper peninsula of Michigan "God's Country," but whenever we went up there, my mother couldn't wait to cross the Mackinac Bridge and get back to the lower peninsula.

Mom felt as though the U.P. was too secluded and desolate with hardly anything there except trees. That's really what makes it so beautiful—extensive forests and big rolling hills. If it weren't so cold in the winter, it would have been an excellent place for me to retire. However, I wanted more than a week and a half of summer every year.

As Rick's first semester came to a close, my dad drove up to pick him up for Christmas break, which was a good eight to nine-hour trip. Not being one to ever turn away from having fun with friends, my brother and his buddies got some beer and decided it would be a good idea to drive out and uncork a few beverages the night before they went home. He wasn't going back to Northern the next semester, so saying goodbye "appropriately" with buddies was understandable.

As luck would have it, the police got a hold of them on a back road and hauled them off to jail. My brother had to call my dad where he was staying and tell him the "good" news, and Dad had to retrieve him. As Rick later told us, Dad was so mad that the only time they talked the entire way home was when they crossed the bridge, about four hours from where they started, when my dad asked if he was hungry.

I was sitting in a chair when they finally got home. It was late, and I knew I needed to go to bed, but I couldn't until I had the chance to tell my big brother "hello," have my laugh, and I also couldn't wait to see how things played out. Dad and Rick walked into the house. My brother went right to his bedroom, and Dad wore a look that was sure to put the fear of God into anyone. I was disappointed there weren't more fireworks, but when Dad got angry, he didn't have to say anything; you just *knew* it. To this day, Rick says they only opened one beer before they got busted by the police, but I don't buy that one. I'm glad I never created a mess like that for my parents... Uh-huh.

Dad was a hardworking man, working for Ford Motor Company for forty years. He was in the Navy during WWII for a few years, and that, I'm sure, helped shape him into an influential person. He grew up without a father. Ralph Throop died when my dad was five. Dad was as good a man as you'll ever know, and he was respected as much as anyone in town.

The only time I ever heard him curse was when we were at the mall, and it was pouring rain. We dropped Mom off at the door, but he and I searched for a good parking spot. One was just about to become available, so we waited for the people whose spot we wanted to get into their car. It seemed like it took forever, but my dad had the patience of Job.

After fifteen or twenty minutes, they began backing up, and we were relieved. We were going to get a parking spot close to the front door of the mall! But just as they pulled all the way out and left, another car zoomed past us and pulled into that spot. Uh-oh!

Dad got out of our car and yelled, "You son of a bitch!"

I just about freaked out, but the parking spot thieves got out of their vehicle and raced as fast they could into the mall—because it was pouring rain, sure, but probably because they saw my dad and figured they'd picked the wrong guy to make angry. Man, was I scared for them!

My dad was six feet, three inches tall. He weighed two hundred and thirty pounds and could have broken that car in half, preferably with the people still in it. When you shook hands with him, he swallowed your hand in his, and although he was a teddy bear, nobody messed with big Don Throop. Dad also spoiled my mom and worshiped the ground she walked on.

Neva was a stay-at-home mom, but once I got a little older, she worked part-time as a nursery school teacher. Her claim to fame was having taught Kid Rock as well as the children of the Detroit Tigers pitcher, Mickey Lolich. She did the latter in 1968 when Lolich was the Most Valuable Player of the World Series, throwing and winning three games on the mound while hitting a homerun. He was a household name, so it was kind of cool that my mom got to talk with him and his family a couple of times every week.

With that part-time job, Mom was always home by the time we arrived from school, and she had everything under control around the homestead. She was highly involved in my life and the lives of my siblings and was the Room Mother for my class at school every year. There was no doubt about it, we had a great mother. She made sure things were tended to daily—our house was always in order, clothes washed, dinner made every night, and each of the beds was made.

I'm not sure my two youngest sons ever made their beds the last six years they lived at home, but my mom did the job every day while still making sure her husband and kids took priority. When clothes got washed, Mom always hung them on the clothesline to dry since we didn't own a clothes dryer. Most of the neighbors didn't have one either. In the colder months, she used a clothesline downstairs to dry our clothes, but during the warm months, she hung them on the lines in our backyard.

Summer became a social time for the neighborhood ladies, as they'd hang clothes and then sit in the backyard, drinking coffee. As I think about that today, I realize they drank *a lot* of coffee after the work was done, and I wonder what else they had in those cups. Betty, Janet, Zelda, and Neva Throop were the four amigos, and we were fortunate we all lived next door to one another.

Haven't we all been through many situations during our time

growing up and then reminisced about those things, both good and bad?

We played outside all day and went wherever we wanted without fear of anything bad happening to us. Bike rides four or five miles out into the country occurred all the time in the summer, many times taking five to six hours to complete. We just had to explore something new on the way out and back.

The most intriguing trips were the ones where I'd stop at the little creek to goof around. Other kids were there often, and fishing was a mainstay at that location, even though I'm not sure anyone ever caught a fish. The one thing that my best friend at that time, Robby Lahde, did catch was a fishhook in the leg when a cast went awry. We wound up getting it out and continued our fishing adventures without having to run home and cry to Mom before being taken to the doctor.

It's said by many that kids were tougher back then, and I believe that to be the truth. Keep in mind that we were maybe eleven or twelve years old when we made those trips, but it was customary, as were other childhood staples. Drinking out of the hose when we were thirsty always took place, because if we went in the house, Mom might make us stay in and have lunch or something crazy like that. Not coming in until we were called home well after dark frequently happened because the neighborhood kids and I had to play hide-and-seek.

One of the luckiest days of my life as a bit of a lad was when I played with some neighbor kids in one of their barns. For some reason, I left. I hopped on my bike and left, and I must have gone riding with nowhere to go and nothing in mind except riding.

Speaking of riding, I don't see many kids today saying, "I'll be back later. I'm going to ride my bike." They've got better things to do, like play on their $1,000 cell phones and the Video Game Machine—whatever that thing's called.

Anyway, a short time after I left, I heard the fire whistle blow and looked up to see a billowing cloud of smoke coming from down the street. I got the pedals on my bike moving a little quicker and caught a glimpse of a massive fire in the barn we were playing in. I found out that the other guys who were in the barn started playing with matches and burned that barn to the ground.

Their tails got whipped pretty good, I'm sure, but I was off the hook because I wasn't there. I got to play the sweet, innocent child when asked if I was a part of it. Whew!

4

THE MOB?

We didn't have a lot of money growing up, but I never knew that. Times were simpler back then, for the most part, and the material demands didn't seem to be the way they are today. My parents didn't take us out for dinner very often, and we didn't do many extravagant things.

Instead, we "hung out" and watched a lot of television on a black-and-white screen. Once in a blue moon on a Friday, we got treated to dinner at the Peerless Cafe in downtown Romeo. When we finished eating, Dad would hand me a five-dollar bill, and I'd head up to the cash register and pay the bill. Five dollars!

One of our "edge-of-your-seat" family activities was driving downtown and parking in front of the Dime Store to watch cars go by and people walking. I would indeed bug my dad to do that often, and sometimes he'd even break down and give me a dollar to go into the Dime Store. I'd buy a toy of some type, but my favorite was the bag full of little green army men. Going home and having World War III in the family living room was awesome.

During the year, my parents saved enough money to take our family on vacation up to Burt Lake in Indian River, Michigan for a couple of weeks. We rented a cottage right on the lake and didn't have a worry in the world. We also met some great people there, who came back every year around the same time we did. Some of those families became terrific friends even after we stopped going, and we visited them down in southern Michigan. Sadly, as time passed, so did the contacts we'd made.

One of those families was Italian and had some exciting ties to other Italian folks back in Detroit, where their home was. My mom loved telling the story of when four or five sleek black Lincolns showed up at their cottage to pay a visit to their friends. Several of the guys were in suits, and before long, all the adults put two and two together. Me and the other kids? I'm sure we saw a chance to have more kids show up to play with us. We went over to the fancy cars, opened the doors, and sat in them. A suited member of their entourage told me I shouldn't sit in their car, and I didn't argue.

Those people who vacationed with us had interests in a suspicious business back in Detroit that had some entanglement with "celebrities," such as the top two Michigan mob bosses. The business always had controversies with legal issues, and years later, they were busted for organized crime activities.

Whether it was Jimmy Hoffa or Tony Giacalone who showed up at Burt Lake, I don't know, but I wouldn't be surprised. Mom and Dad always said they were extremely friendly and generous, which could have very well resulted in the fact that my dad was a loyal union guy when he worked at Ford Motor Company. Being able to rub shoulders with Hoffa might have been like eating dinner with the President.

5

QUITE THE LEISURELY LIFE

When I got to my latter elementary and early junior high school days, my parents bought a membership to a unique nine-hole golf course called Bruce Hills. It sure wasn't much of a course, but it had a wonderful family feel.

During the summers, Mom dropped me off there in the morning, probably four or five days a week. I played anywhere from eighteen to thirty-six holes with my best friend, Robby, whose family also had a membership. After work, Dad came out, and he and I played nine more holes. Keep in mind that we didn't take golf carts back then, but walked the entire time. Taking a carriage wasn't even discussed. We got the legs moving up and down the fairways, and sometimes into the woods, where our balls occasionally flew.

Snowmobiles were allowed to drive on the course in the winter, and at times, my parents were asked to come out and manage the site on the weekend. That came with perks. I could take one of the course's snowmobiles and ride all night.

There I was, in junior high school, riding at night, over frozen ponds with the only light being that of the moon, coming upon other snowmobilers and having no idea who they were, and leaving the course property to venture into some unknown field—all at the age of twelve. Try to imagine parents allowing their kids to do that today; they'd be hauled off to prison for child abuse and neglect. Most parents embraced their kids' adventurous spirits, and they didn't have to worry about all the stuff parents worry about now.

After we played golf in the summer, I went home and had dinner around the table like other families did at that time. It might have been the only time I ate the peas on my plate so that I could go down to the Congregational Church and play basketball for a couple of hours. I mostly tried to hide my vegetables in the mashed potatoes so Mom thought I ate them. Playing with Marvin, another kid also named Marvin, Donnell, Zach, and the other guys who showed up made for some intense playground hoops. I usually got harassed the most, but it was a great learning experience.

6

THE NEIGHBORHOOD

Our neighborhood was unique. The Perrys, Burkes, Shoemakers, Rashids, Dahns, Shanlians, Lahdes, Gillespies, and Lees were part of that neighborhood and those whose children I played with. The kids in those families consisted of mostly boys, but there were some girls as well.

We had entertainment in so many fashions that our kids today aren't able to enjoy and experience. Homerun derby, going to the school playground, trying to form garage bands (even though none of us could play an instrument), swimming in the Perrys' pool, and other things kept us outside most of the time. At night, we played hide-and-seek and other games that allowed us to be kids. Everything we did was fun and didn't cause trouble.

Well, almost everything...

The one creative event on the border of disorder was a game we called "Pull." One person stood on one side of the street with someone else on the other, both kids directly across from each other. Each was reasonably close to the road, and when a car came by, we yelled, "Pull!" and make it look like we were pulling something that might hit the vehicle when actually there was nothing.

It was enough to startle the driver and make them squeal their tires to a stop. We'd then run like crazy to get away so the person in the car couldn't catch us, although we did have a few close calls. It was a quiet street where the speed limit was twenty-five, so thankfully, nobody ever got into an accident.

A lot of summer nights featured times when we'd "sleep out." During the day, we prepared our tents, which consisted of taking out some old blankets and sheets and hanging them over the clothesline. We loaded up on snacks—a bottle of pop and homemade popcorn was a must—and then everyone settled in for the night.

I guess we made it through the night outside around twenty-five percent of the time. A spooky noise or something that scared us usually made us run inside. Sometimes, we got in a fight with someone else in the tent, it rained, or the occasional skunk that walked by and spread his not-so-pleasant odor were other factors.

If you're from Romeo, you know exactly when the most crucial time of the year is: Labor Day and the Michigan Peach Festival! I could write an entire book on those events. The fun that we had was second to none. Those weekends drew in perhaps an additional 100,000 out-of-towners to a town of about 4,000 people.

The events went from Friday to Monday, and three parades ran through the town. We even had a carnival that included some sketchy rides, put together with, I think, Elmer's glue. Cookouts, seeing friends all over town, and having fun were simple ways of enjoying the festive atmosphere.

In the mid-'60s, neighbors and many others in town went down to the beer tent during the Peach Festival, on either one night or all of the nights. Hundreds of people were having fun, for the most part, but with that many people gathered and the amount of beer being consumed, we always had some half-brains looking for trouble. And drink they did.

Every year, new stories and tales were created, thanks to the biggest events in town. Perhaps one of the most memorable came from a time when I was too young for the beer tent.

I stayed at our house along with some neighbor kids. That night, the adults came home, making for another loud return. There were probably a half-dozen neighbors along with one guy, who was a stranger. He was drunk, and his friends had left him behind at the beer tent. The only problem was that he lived about a half-hour away. Lying on the side of the street because he had no ride, my parents said he could sleep on our back porch. Dad... you kidding me?

The night went fine, and all the neighbors returned for breakfast the next morning. We all did our best not to step on whatever the guy's name was snoozing in the middle of the back porch. After about twenty minutes, he woke up and had zero clue about where he was, but he accepted some of my dad's bacon and eggs.

After breakfast, somebody thought it was a good idea to take him home, but they chose my sister and a friend of hers to do it. Never forgetting about safety, my mom sent me and a friend, both of us about ten or eleven years old, to go with them. Let's see... two young ladies and two pre-teens in a car with a guy nobody knew and looked like he'd just come off of a high night of drinking. Wait —he *had* just come off a night-before-bender! Believe it or not, we made it and successfully dropped the man off.

Amazingly, again, I didn't die.

7

ALMOST AN ADULT

Great neighborhood things happened for my friends and me when we were young, mainly in the sixth grade and under the teen years. Once we got to junior high school, there was more to do and new friends were made. There was still time to hang out during the summer. Our parents socialized with each other quite often, so we naturally hung out when they did.

What was crazy and a little depressing is that we never hung out with one another by the time we got to high school. We all seemed to acquire new interests and new friends; some of us moved away, and some took different directions in life. Having no cell phones, Facebook, Twitter, or all the other things available today made it difficult to communicate unless we made an effort to do so.

As a sixth-grade student at North Grade School in Romeo, I had a teacher named Harry Foltz, who kids liked but also feared. He was a tall guy, almost as tall as I was, and had one of those tough-sounding voices.

On one unforgettable day, he told me to be quiet, but within thirty seconds, I was talking again. The look on his face told me he wasn't about to present me with the "Student Of The Day" award.

Instead, Mr. Foltz told me to step out into the hall, where my backside met with his wooden paddle. One whack, two whacks, three whacks, and my posture was not what it had been five minutes earlier that day, but I was an attentive student after that experience.

I also suffered the wrath of Miss Wheeler's paddle in middle school, although I can't remember what caused it. What I can tell you is that I wound up getting A's in her class afterward, as my attention level magically improved. I also never spoke a word about it to my parents; I desperately wanted to see my next birthday. Can you imagine that in today's times? No more job for that teacher!

I'm one of those crazy idealists that believe school staff not only have a right but a responsibility to defend themselves and other students, which might include physical contact. I'd be interested to know how many kids that got the paddle "back in the day" suffered life-long effects. I'd also be interested to see how many of those that got paddled learned *not* to do something they shouldn't. I think I know which result happened overwhelmingly.

One central area gobbled up more of my time than anything else. Sports! As I grew throughout my childhood, I played sports and watched them. I followed sports, listened to them on the radio, went to all the events—I breathed sports.

I read the sports section of the newspaper every day and have done so since I learned to read. Somebody put all the little league statistics in our local newspaper each week and summarized every game, and I understand now what a benefit that was. Heck, today, there are hardly any newspapers out there, and in many cases, you can't find any high school games outlined.

I watched every sporting event on TV—yes, every sports show there was—because there weren't many to watch, mainly because we only had three channels.

Walking to the high school on cold, snowy Saturday mornings to play in Coach Barr's Saturday morning basketball program and playing on the high school court for an hour was a thrill!

I experienced a lot in those years, so much that there are simply too many memories to include. Remember, there weren't any travel teams or youth leagues like you see now, but it was still sports, sports, and more sports. It was fairly innocent, as the teams were coached by somebody's father. Little league baseball with my dad as our coach was an incredible experience. I never realized at the time how lucky I was to have that happen.

8

JUNIOR HIGH SCHOOL YEARS

Even though I was involved in sports, I began taking an interest in the fairer sex. I also became a member of the student council and was probably the Most Valuable Player at seconding motions made by members much smarter than me. Yep, I was a subpar student council member, and I don't think I ever contributed much, but it was fun getting out of class for the meetings. There were also a decent number of good-looking girls, which made it hard to concentrate on what was going on.

One of our meetings ended early, and we had about fifteen minutes before class was over; Band class for me. Most of us didn't go back to our classes, but I was the only one ditching Band, and the teacher, Mr. Middleton, noticed. After school, a few kids found me and told me Mr. Middleton was upset. It was Friday, so I worried about it all weekend.

When it came to going to that class on Monday, I knew I was in serious trouble. I entered the band room and saw Mr. Middleton in his office. He yelled, "Throop!"

I was close to crying as I walked into his office, feeling it might be my last day on Earth. Even though I was expecting the worst, he sat me down, smiled at me, and said, "I have an idea for you." He then told me he wanted me to experiment with playing the tuba.

I played the snare drum, but I didn't like it, which meant I never practiced. But that intuitive teacher knew I wasn't fond of drums, so instead of punishing me, he found a way to encourage me by trying something different. And so, I was off the drum and began playing the tuba.

Guess what? I found it to be kind of fun, so I practiced a great deal and became a decent tuba player. Bill Middleton was an excellent teacher. I even wound up playing tuba in high school, but I didn't continue with the student council.

Girls aside, I always thought the best part of being on the student council was the end-of-the-year dinner our advisor treated us to, where we could order anything we wanted from the menu. That kept me participating through my middle school years, but as I got older, I lost interest. That free dinner just wasn't as important anymore.

Being tall for my age led me down the path of getting more serious about playing basketball. I played a lot in the driveway with neighborhood kids, but one thing I did to get better was a little goofy. I'd hop on my bike and ride out to the little creek, which wasn't uncommon for me to do. The difference was I'd dribble a basketball all the way there and back while on my bike. That was no easy task!

After I did it for quite some time and got good at it, I started doing it in the dark, which made it difficult to see the ball. I had to rely on the ball's feel. There were times I bounced the ball off a bike pedal or a spot in the road that sent it somewhere I'd have to chase it down, but after a while, it became second nature to ride all the way to the creek and back without a single mistake. It paid off big dividends in high school and college, as I was the one who helped bring the ball down when the other team pressed us at both levels. People who play center position aren't typically the players doing that, but that creek practice got me to that point.

During junior high, I made a whole new set of friends. I wasn't only around the neighborhood North Grade Elementary School kids. In fact, I rarely saw any of the kids I was friends with at North Grade. It was also the first time we didn't have the same teacher all day long. We had to travel from room to room. We were big stuff!

Walking past the teacher's lounge; now that was interesting...

Each time the door was opened, thick plumes of cigarette smoke flowed from the room. Again, those were the "good old days," and seeing teachers smoke was not unusual. I remember coming home one day after watching a teacher pour a little alcohol into their coffee. I mentioned it to my parents in casual conversation and their reaction was, "Well, keeping all you kids in line is a tough job."

Always being involved in some sport was my life, and it pretty much revolved around playing, watching, and keeping up with different teams. Without question, my favorite team was—as is to this day—the Detroit Tigers. Al Kaline, Mickey Lolich, Willie Horton, and the rest of the players were like gods to me.

The Tigers had a magical year while I was in middle school during the summer of 1968, but the summer of '67 was a dark time for Detroit. The city went through one of the most negative things it ever has, a time of great racial divide and severe rioting. It was a scary and defining moment and one that people remember to this day.

Even though we lived about a half-hour from the city, things in Romeo were tense. We didn't have a super large minority population, but enough to know that they were on edge as well. Watching our local police—there was only one police car in town at the time—ride around with helmets just seemed off.

The Tigers won the 1968 pennant, and it provided healing for the city. Successful sports teams at any level bring people together in a positive way. The World Series that year was against the St. Louis Cardinals, and they had a unit that many future Hall of Fame players were a part of.

Bob Gibson was the pitcher for the Cardinals for Game One of the Series, and our poor Tigers didn't have a chance. Gibson struck out seventeen batters, and we were defeated 4-0. However, after that game, my dad informed me that if the Tigers were to make it to the fifth game, which would be in Detroit, he and I were going, as he secured tickets from someone. Thank goodness the Tigers *did* win one of the first four games, which meant the Series was coming back to Detroit for Game Five!

On the day of the game, Dad came to get me out of the school early, but the principal was not going to allow it for such a reason as going to a baseball game. He wasn't a bad guy, but he felt like students should be in school instead of going to games. I understand that feeling, but it was the World Series, and my dad wasn't going to have it any other way. He took me out of school anyway, and we went to the game.

We parked on 12th Street, where much of the rioting from the year before took place, and we walked to Tiger Stadium. Wow... What an environment! Our seats were in the lower level of the center field bleachers, which turned out to be exciting seats.

The National Anthem was sung from centerfield by a man named Jose Feliciano, and his rendition was as uncommon as it has ever been. He tried to jazz it up but ended up singing a different melody than anyone had ever heard before. We were surrounded by all colors, shapes, and sizes of people that day, and not one of them thought it was appropriate. There was nothing "wrong" with his style, but the National Anthem was always sung in its traditional way, so hearing it otherwise was quite a shocker for everyone.

Oh, well. Play ball!

The game was exciting, and to be there was more than a tad bit of fun. We wound up beating St. Louis by a score of 5-3 behind the superb pitching of Mickey Lolich and an essential play by catcher Bill Freehan, who threw out their speedster Lou Brock as he tried to steal second base for the first time in the Series. It seemed to get the juices flowing, and we came back to win the Series in seven games. Lolich was the World Series MVP and hero; he won three of our four games, pitching and even hitting a memorable homerun.

When it was over, he brought his kids to my mom's nursery school, like usual, and got inundated with people while there. He gave my mom several autographed pictures, but for the life of me, I have no idea what happened to them. Sadly, they probably wound up going into the same trash cans as the rookie baseball cards of Roberto Clemente and Nolan Ryan.

Junior High was also the first time I got to participate in real sports teams other than little league baseball. The school had football, basketball, and baseball teams when we got into the ninth grade, giving many of us a chance to play for one of my lifelong mentors and friends to this day, Jim Feldkamp.

At one of our basketball practices, we decided to wear tape around our wrists to mimic the sweatbands that had become a "cool" trend in the NBA. We got about halfway through the practice, and Coach Feldkamp called us together and stated that he felt sorry for all of us due to the fact that we had wrist problems, evident from the tape we were wearing. He said he felt the need to strengthen our wrists, so we all did push-ups for what felt like a year. The message was sent loud and clear that we would do things *his* way. We didn't wear tape again.

Because students had to be enrolled in the senior high school to move up to a different team, freshmen had to play on the freshmen team. I was happy that it was that way. The guys in that class were special, and every football, basketball, and baseball team we had in junior high and all the way up through high school won a lot. We had many thrilling experiences, and it indwelled us with the desire to win even more.

Football season came and brought with it our first real team. It was different! Ernie Maule was our coach, as he had been the ninth-grade coach for many years. I was the team's wide receiver, and we were pretty good.

In the last game of the year, we played Rochester, which was an outstanding team. Nobody scored for most of the game. Every time we snapped the ball, our quarterback got hit. Late in the fourth quarter, an epic play named the Mauly Special was called. It was well-known from year to year, involving—well, I don't know. All I remember is that I was supposed to catch the ball. Amazingly, our quarterback, Dave Maxwell, threw it to me and I caught it. I ran toward the endzone with a ten-yard lead, but with my speed, it was erased in a hurry. Thankfully, I made it to the goal line, and we won 6-0.

The best part of that game happened when we got back to school. I got my first kiss from a cheerleader. I couldn't run away fast enough. Feelings of fear and weirdness hit me upside the head. It felt like my life was all different now. I was a man! Ha.

We started that basketball season by losing our first two games. However, Coach Feldkamp somehow got us playing better as a team, and we wound up winning the rest of our games. I was the Most Valuable Player, but it didn't mean much because our team was developing as a whole, and we knew we were in for good things. Yes, we were.

Spring came, and so did baseball. Again, we had an excellent team. I played first base and pitched a little. At the end of the year, I was named captain and was determined to continue getting ready for high school sports. Not science, math, or geography, but sports.

After the season but before school was over brought about the first time I drank a beer. It was not terrific! However, peer pressure had me drink a few more of them.

I also went to my first dance, which was a Sadie Hawkins dance, where a girl asks a guy to go. Two girls wanted to ask me, so I told a friend that the first to ask was the one I'd go with. Well, like an idiot, my date and I got to the door, and I let her pay for both of us. I don't think she was happy about that, but it might have given me an extra fifty cents for a candy bar, so what the heck.

Once we got inside, she ditched me, and I wound up with the other girl, who I asked to "go with me" later that night. Saturday, a buddy and I got a ring that cost a dollar and I gave it to her Monday at school. I don't think I ever talked to her again after that.

Junior high romances... You have to love them.

9

HIGH SCHOOL

When we took those massive steps from junior high to senior high school, many great things were ahead of me. In no way am I saying how great I was, but I hung out with all the athletes, and I was popular among the other kids. They knew who I was, and being the tallest kid in school and excelling in athletics made it that way.

Now that I've had that experience, I'll say that the more popular you are in high school, the more stupid decisions you make. That's the excuse I'm using, anyway.

My best buddy, Brian Woodhouse, was an excellent baseball player. He wound up playing college baseball after graduation while I headed in the basketball direction. The number of stories I could tell about me and Brian could fill another book so I won't even try, nor will I implicate the two of us. Our tales never involved anything too serious, but without question, there are a couple of interesting PG (okay, maybe PG-13) ones that I'll share. No use in getting into the R-rated stories!

He and I spent the night at each other's house quite often. Brian lived on 27 Mile Road, out in the country, and I lived in town on Bailey Street. Brian had a couple of older brothers who were "adventurous," and they occasionally helped us garner a little of "the suds."

Right up there with the worst laws that Michigan may have ever passed was when the legislature voted to lower the age for the right to buy and consume alcohol to eighteen years old. This was during the Vietnam War. Even though my friends and I weren't aware of the war's negative magnitude—we were always busy playing sports and chasing girls—the country was obviously in a state of major change and revolt.

Many felt that if our boys were old enough to go overseas and fight for their country and possibly die, they were old enough to buy and drink alcohol. Neither was a good decision. It sounded good on the surface, but it was a terrible law that saw alcohol-related accidents and other nasty scenarios increase because of alcohol's easy availability.

I remember walking by my classmates' lockers and often seeing a six-pack of Miller High Life beer or a little bottle of some liquor. I never did that, but I always laughed when I saw others doing it, which was maybe ten or so times. Don't get me wrong—the group of people I hung with drank our share from the brown bottle, but we tried to be a little more discreet. However, some of "The Boys" who played other sports also played intramural basketball. I was on the basketball team, but I'll never forget that the intramural guys had a team that called themselves the Brown Bottled Bombers. How's that for being discreet!

I spent the night at Brian's house one night while we were seniors in high school. His parents weren't in town. That alone was a recipe for disaster and mischief, and we took full advantage of it. Brian's older brother Danny was a big, tough son of a gun, and he liked motorcycles. There were two bikes at the house as well as some shotguns they used for hunting.

We started the night by shooting guns out in the field after a couple of Wiedeman beers (the cans looked just like a Budweiser can, so it was commonly referred to as Polish Bud). I essentially had no experience with guns. We were lucky; only a couple of windows were broken that night.

A while later, a couple of the fairer sex came out to the house, and we hopped on those motorcycles—me with no motorcycle experience, all of us with no helmets—and drove up and down 27 Mile Road with the girls on the back, driving at high rates of speed. Again, we were lucky, to say the least. It's not something I could ever imagine doing today, and definitely a stupid choice. We were fortunate not to have killed ourselves or someone else. What a couple of idiots!

Brian had another brother, Mike, who was a senior on the basketball team when I was a sophomore on the team. I looked up to Mike. He was an outstanding athlete and seemed to always be able to smooth-talk the ladies while still being genuinely nice to me, yet consistently trying to beat the snot out of Brian. I thought Mike would blow a gasket when he got home and found out what we were doing. But...

Amazingly, I didn't die.

Why had I been given another pass, once again, in my continual physical escapades based on dumb choices?

At some point in that era of oh-so-solid-decision-making, my parents bought a new Ford Maverick automobile, an average vehicle, but one that cost under $2,000. It was my parents' car, but once I could drive, it became mine as long as my parents didn't need it. It was all black, with a three-in-the-tree shifter. Anyone under twenty-five reading this may ask, "What's three-in-the-tree mean, and what's a shifter?" Ask your parents, or maybe even your grandparents.

I rode that car hard, but on one particular night while I was out with three or four people, I decided I wanted to be extra cool. I got up to a good speed and made a sharp right turn, making the car lean heavily. The tires screeched as loud as anyone had ever heard! How that car didn't flip the three different times I did that, I have no idea.

But you know what? Amazingly, I didn't die. Again.

My friends were significant to me in high school, and I had a lot of them. Several of us guys that hung around together were called "The Boys," like a little gang or something. We never caused harm to anyone and all we wanted to do was have fun. It didn't seem to matter if there were three of us or twenty. We all considered ourselves The Boys.

There might be five guys at one location, three at another, and eight somewhere else. People still said, "There are The Boys!" Also, nobody quite knew who was in The Boys—even if you were part of it—as there was no roster, no membership, and nothing more than a group of "let's have fun" guys. Anybody was welcome.

Some of our worst offenses were being out after curfew by fifteen minutes and having to answer for ourselves, and having a Schlitz or two on occasion. Well... maybe on several occasions. I know many teachers and coaches were suspicious of us, but since most of The Boys were athletes, we won a ton of championships for our sports teams.

Those guys meant so much to me. Even though I haven't seen most of them in decades, I still consider them great friends. Gosh, now I kind of feel like crying.

In my sophomore year, I played football. Once again, we had a good team. I scored a touchdown just about every game. However, I was looking forward to basketball season.

At the first practice, I started with our J.V. team, but after my first layup of that first practice, Coach Barr told me to go to the other end of the floor with the varsity guys. Wow! What a thrill. I was nervous, but I had hoped I'd make the varsity team, so being there was a dream come true.

It was an excellent year for us. We went 17-0 during and won the conference. When we got to the first game of the state tournament, we played a mediocre team and got beat. What a tragedy!

Being a part of that team with the older guys meant I could hang out with the seniors. One night, a couple of the National Merit scholars took me to a place near Detroit called the Rumpus Room. I rarely had my identification checked. I was tall and the drinking age was eighteen, so I got in with no problem. The girls dancing there had me wondering what I had been missing all my life. You guessed it, it was one of "those" places.

Baseball season came, and I got placed at first base again. I was also a pitcher on the J.V. team. Sadly, it would be my last year of playing both football and baseball. I look back with tremendous regret at not having played more baseball. I wasn't the best player, but I was decent. My issue wasn't with the sport, but with the varsity coach. I believed he was morally bankrupt and had done something to my dad that was unforgivable.

We had a beautiful new blue Ford Galaxie 500 convertible car, but the coach had the exact vehicle. He was out in the country with a woman who wasn't his wife, and to save his skin, he told everyone it was my dad's car and not his. Talk about disgusting. I wanted nothing to do with him after that. I feel he would have treated me fairly, but I didn't want to be around him. As it turns out, the baseball team made it to the state finals during my senior year, so obviously, they didn't miss me too much.

Things got interesting my sophomore year. The recruiting process started. I would be deciding where to play college basketball!

I received letters almost every day while I was in high school. The first came from Clemson University, where they detailed the opportunity of a full four-year full-ride scholarship that would run $15,000. Today, that amount might not even be able to pay for one semester of in-state schooling, much less an out-of-state student, but my parents were giddy. They knew that I might have a real shot to play college basketball *without* having to pay for me to go to school.

I figured I had a good chance of landing a scholarship because I played basketball all the time, in the driveway during rainstorms and in the winter months, even if I had to shovel snow to do so, and I was good. Youth basketball leagues and organized basketball events weren't even a blip on the radar back then, so we had to make things happen ourselves and find ways to practice and improve.

I knew I was finally terrific when I played against Wilt Chamberlain and Lew Alcindor (who later changed his name to Kareem Abdul-Jabbar), and I always beat them. Of course, they weren't physically there, but I pretended they were and I smoked them. When I blocked Wilt's shot and sent it into the snowbank, I heard the crowd roar and chant my name. Yep, I was the man!

As I entered my sophomore year, I went to basketball camp at Western Michigan University. Sports camps weren't popular then, but it was an excellent experience for me despite getting homesick being three hours away from Mommy and Daddy!

Although Western was where my sister graduated from and we'd been there several times, the drive seemed to take forever on the day my parents dropped me off at camp. While there, I stayed at the home of Eldon Miller, who was the head coach at Western. I think that might have been an illegal thing to do, but he housed me, fed me, brought me to camp, and took care of me for the week. Coach Miller is one of the finest people I've ever known, and his ability to recruit athletes and talk to parents while still directing his influence toward kids was outstanding.

I received letters of interest from over 150 schools. Getting a letter doesn't mean you're getting recruited, but it simply means they know who you are, you're on their radar, and the rest is up to you. They'll listen for your name in the future.

It always frustrated me when I got into my professional career that parents told everyone they knew that their child was getting recruited by a school when they received a letter. I know it was just them being proud parents, but it's one thing that has caused some of the issues we deal with in high school athletics today. It's not terrible for parents to get excited, but it adds to misnomers of how good their kids are.

The first time I flew in an airplane, I headed to my visit to Georgetown University in Washington D.C., where legendary Coach John Thompson was the head coach. He was at the beginning of building that program, where he did an excellent job with the success they had over the years.

I only got to spend one afternoon with him. The assistant coach and the players dominated most of my time, but on the afternoon we spent together, he bought me lunch, we ate in a park, and he and I saw the White House. It was pretty overwhelming—I thought we were only going to look at it, but when he identified himself, we drove right in.

When the weekend was over and it was time for me to fly home, he came to my room to pick me up. One of the recruiting tactics he used was bringing a Georgetown uniform, laying it on the bed, and telling me how great I would look in it. He then said that he was going to use the restroom but again stated how great I'd look in the uniform.

Being a stupid high school kid, I felt good about what he said and thought nothing else of it. But when he came out of the restroom, he looked at the uniform, looked at me, and then said that he was going *back* into the bathroom and firmly reiterated that I *would* look great in the uniform. I'm not the sharpest tool in the shed, but I finally got the hint, grabbed the uniform, and shoved it in my suitcase before we left for the airport.

Another memorable visit was when I went to Colorado State. That was a lot of fun, and I'll leave most of it at that. It was a stunning campus, and being next to the Rocky Mountains in Fort Collins was scenic. After I got picked up at the airport by the assistant coach and his friend, we went to dinner. When dinner was over, we went to a concert along with a couple of other team players.

After about twenty minutes, the coach told me what the plans for the morning were and that he'd pick me up. He and the other players started to leave, and I asked how I was to get home that night. Well, the coach's friend was a girl, and she took me home. No further information is available. The team members who were there could do nothing but laugh the following day when I saw them.

Our home phone always seemed to be ringing, with another coach calling with interest in me. It was fun at first, but after a while, it became a pain in the neck and I felt tons of pressure. My parents and I took turns answering the phone. Sometimes they shielded me, saying I wasn't home if I didn't want to talk to anyone.

At one point, one of the coaches from Western Michigan came to the house and while he was there, the head coach at Central Michigan University stopped by unannounced, which put both of them there at the same time. Our house wasn't huge, so there was no getting around trying to balance things out.

After a couple of hours, the CMU coach left, and Coach Shilts from Western and brought in some game film to watch. They'd both tried to outlast the other, but Coach Shilts undoubtedly was not going to bring in game film and watch it with WMU's biggest rival sitting in the same living room. My dad had to get up at 5:00 in the morning for work, so at midnight, he went to bed with Coach Shilts leaving a little while after that.

I played on the golf team my senior year, and a coach from an SEC school came out to the golf course one fall day and tracked me down during one of our high school matches. He followed me around the entire time, which was both impressive and weird. He even came to the house after the match. He visited with us for about an hour and then asked me to go outside with him as he left. When we got to his car, he opened the trunk and showed me a substantial amount of money, somewhere in the thousands of dollars range, and said it could be mine if he left that night with my commitment to attend his school.

As the son of a factory worker and part-time nursery school teacher, I was overwhelmed. I didn't say yes, but I didn't get the cash either. Had I any brains at the time, I should have told him I'd strongly consider their school if I could have half the money. That would have bought me a lot of golf balls and Wiedemans!

My final choices of schools came down to Western Michigan, Colorado State (gee, I wonder why), Central Michigan, Georgetown, and Toledo. At the time, I wanted to go into business and possibly be a large hotel manager, so having a good business school was important. My sister had gone to Western and I had the summer camp background with Eldon Miller, who I liked. It seemed like all of those factors led me to choosing WMU. Western was a program on the rise with Eldon there. I had a good second visit and was able to bring my buddy Brian along on that trip.

When I think back on those years and to one couple I know that went through some tough times, my parents immediately come to mind. They've been through the Great Depression, gone through

World War II, and dealt with children of the '60s and '70s that changed the world so fast even Houdini would probably be impressed by their almost supersonic pace. The latter might have just been the most challenging time of all for them!

When you think of what they saw during their lives, it's nothing short of incredible. I can only wonder about the level of stress they had to go through compared to what we Boomers have seen, and especially what our children have seen.

Folks, it's a darn good place to be, this old United States of America, with all its opportunities to succeed if you truly want to. Yes, that's true for *whoever* wants it.

And *thank you* to those who allowed me to remain free, to have what I want to have, think how I like to think, and say what I want to say—for the most part, as long as those comments aren't so whacked out that they'd be pronounced as inappropriate.

10

SEE YA', ROMEO. HELLO, KALAMAZOO!

G oing off to college is an intimidating thing for kids, but I wasn't nervous at all. I was excited about what was ahead of me. Basketball made it that way.

My roommate was a guy named Kevin McSkimming, and to this day, we're still great friends. We hit it off from the start. We ordered a pizza on our first night at school, and two traditions began.

First, Kevin always read *The Sporting News* while he had pizza. That publication was full of baseball news, which we both liked. That happened all four years of living together, and if there wasn't a *Sporting News* around, he'd wait to eat his pizza until we got back to the dorm with one. It fondly became known as *The Pizza News*.

Second, I had a strange habit of eating a piece of pizza, except for the crust. I'd put that piece of crust back in the box in the same spot its slice came from. When I had eaten my pizza, I'd go back and eat the circle of crusts in the same order I had eaten the original slice. Talk about obsessive-compulsiveness! Weird, I know.

We never shared a pizza, as that seemed ridiculous. During our junior years in college, we ordered so many pizzas that Domino's started calling us around 8:00 to see if any of the four of us who lived in the dorm suite wanted any, which more times than not, we did.

11

THE RAT PATROL

Mine and Kevin's suitemates were Mike Reardon and Mark Rayner, but Kevin, Mike, and I were running mates for all four years and certainly had our share of memorable experiences. If one was going to a party or the store, the others were bound to follow. We couldn't let one of us act as though we weren't part of the threesome and miss something exciting that might happen. Mark Rayner was probably the smartest one of the bunch; he didn't do most of the things we did. He's turned into a great husband and father.

Without question, the incident that gave me the most notoriety took place during the first semester of my freshmen year.

Finding a class for the first time on the first day of college is pretty humbling. An entirely new season of life was upon me and walking to a class that seemed like it was ten miles away wasn't pleasurable, especially when I was there to play hoops.

On that first day of Psychology 150, I found out we were required to train a rat how to drink water out of a little cup, which meant going to our rat's cage, picking it up, and putting it in a glass box. About a week into the awful experience, I picked up my giant white rat, and it bit me. By instinct, I tossed the rat against the glass box. A graduate assistant saw me do it and deducted ten points from my grade.

What the heck? I was the victim, but I got in trouble?! I was not a happy camper.

When class was over, I went back to the dorm and the guys laughed, at my expense, of course. I was ticked! They gave me the nickname "Rat," and it stuck throughout my entire college career. Rat this, Rat that. Nobody that knew me called me Marc, and to this day, my basketball teammates call me Rat.

Having a well-decorated dorm room was a necessary part of the college experience, and the things that decorated rooms were sometimes a little bizarre. We were just stupid freshmen who didn't have a clue about that stuff, so our room looked bleak and plain early into our freshman year

One weekend, everyone went back to their hometowns except for me and one of the other guys on the team who lived next door to us in the dorm, sophomore Tom Cutter. "Big Cut" was one of the most laid-back guys you'd ever meet. He was first-team All-Conference, first-team All-Regional in the NCAA tournament and was drafted by the Cleveland Cavaliers. Tom is in the WMU Hall of Fame.

On that memorable weekend, we thought it would be a good idea to make life a little easier for both our room and his. How did we do that? By not having to take the garbage out as often. We made the trek to the McDonalds about a mile behind our dorm, and, like a couple of idiots, we grabbed two of their large garbage cans to eliminate the need for us to have to dump our trash all the time.

McDonald's garbage cans were one of those "not everybody has one of those" prestigious moments. Everybody commented on them when they walked in our rooms. As we learned later, not dumping the garbage for a month wasn't the wisest thing to do. A bad idea? Yes! The odor was awful. Lesson learned.

With all of the changes we witnessed growing up, perhaps the "most influential" was the music. Rock and Roll and Disco were the sounds kids embraced and couldn't get enough of. Plus, some songs had meaning to them. Others you sang and didn't care if they had meaning or not. We listened to the music, danced to the music, and headbanged to the music.

Rock and Roll was my favorite, and still is, even though it's now called "Classic Rock." Led Zeppelin, Aerosmith, Bachman Turner Overdrive, CCR, Lynyrd Skynyrd, and so many other groups were in their prime, and I was fortunate to grow up in that era with them. However, I sure did my share of moving my feet to the Disco scene, especially out at Coral Gables in Kalamazoo, the bar all the college kids went to, especially on Flaming Hog night.

We had to arrive an hour before it opened up or we couldn't get in. The cover charge was somewhere around two dollars but we received four tickets, each good for a bottle of long-neck Stroh's beer. We were able to purchase additional tickets, so ten dollars bought us a night of fun.

As an "all that" in high school, it was eye-opening to see that I was just another player in college, and it didn't take me long to realize that. When playing a sport at that level, the school pretty much owns you and works you in more complex ways than you can imagine.

We were required to take a class called Physical Fitness that conveniently ended on Friday and before official practice started in the fall, and it only had basketball players in it. The course was only fifty minutes long, so how bad could it be? Well, it was fifty minutes of nonstop "without a ball" drill work that left us spent when it was over. Once basketball season started, that class ceased to exist.

Freshman team newcomers sometimes fell victim to pranks. On the first practice of my college career, I was running across a lane, trying to get open and get the ball. Out of nowhere, Paul Griffin grabbed me and threw me to the floor. Paul was our starting forward and went on to play in the NBA for several years. It took me a second to get up off the floor, only to see my coaches chuckling. *Welcome to college basketball, rookie.*

My freshman year was indeed a lot of fun. We went 16-10, and we would have had a chance to win the conference championship if it hadn't been for a guy named Denny Parks from Central Michigan

University. He threw a shot up from the corner, over his shoulder while he was falling out of bounds at the buzzer. They beat us by two! Central was our biggest rival and still is today, so the loss made it that much more difficult to swallow.

They had a great team with Dan Roundfield, Ben Poquette, and Jimmy McElroy, who all went on to have excellent careers in the NBA. Parks was the point guard, while Leonard Drake was their other guard. Leonard and I became friends after graduation, and he became a coach in our area.

I had limited playing time that first year, which, at times, was challenging to handle, but the coaches and other players helped. The team's makeup made it relatively easy. We all had the right mindset of wanting to win instead of worrying about individual accomplishments.

Jim Kurzen was our point guard, and Jeff Tyson was the other guard. Jimmy Harvey played as a small forward and Tom Cutter was the power forward. Paul Griffin was our forward/center and "the name" on the team at that point. Cutter was a sophomore, but everyone else was a junior, so the chances of me playing a lot the following year was going to be tough again.

One of the most exciting games came when we hosted nationally-ranked Notre Dame at home about two-thirds of the way through the year. That was a bizarre game. One of the officials went down early in the game with a sprained ankle. Another alternate official was available, but Notre Dame's coach, Digger Phelps, wouldn't agree to use him.

Remember, back then, there were only two officials in a game, so we wound up playing with one ref for almost the entire game. Digger's logic was that he felt his team was more physical than we were, so playing with one official would lessen the likelihood of seeing all the pushing and fouling going taking place. It almost backfired on Digger, as it was a two-point win for the Fighting Irish, and we were the more aggressive team. That was the last time Notre Dame came to Western.

My first year in college was a great experience. We had a great team, my grades were decent, and I seemed to be relatively focused on essential things. Sure, I did the stereotypical first-year "college things," too, but overall, it was a successful year.

We arrived home from the last game of the season during the tail end of spring break. Mike Reardon, myself, and a teammate, Boyd Breece (Breezly was his nickname) decided to celebrate. We went to the store and bought a couple of cases of beer, and then went back to the room and played Buck Euchre. The game is the same as Euchre but easily played with three players.

Some of you may be saying, "What the heck is Euchre?"

Well, it's a card game, but one of those you might call a Michigan thing. We ended up playing for thirty-six straight hours and drank all the beer… which is why we stopped, or we may have still been there playing today!

TRAVELING THE WORLD

W hen school ended in the spring, our team took a trip to Europe to play against teams over there, but more importantly, it allowed our team to gel. We went eight wins and no losses during our time there, and everybody felt the following year was going to be unique.

One thing I learned there is that there's no place like the USA! That trip was memorable in so many ways, and it never ceased for a bit of fun. Europe seemed about thirty years behind America. Even today, I have no desire to go overseas. We've got too much to offer here.

Upon arrival in Finland, our first stop, about eight of us went to a quaint restaurant to eat and order some beer. Wouldn't you know it? The coaches walked in, and I remember Eldon saying, "Boys, don't try to drink all the beer in the world because I've tried it, and it can't be done." In other words, "Please don't be stupid!" which was something we often were.

We got to meet with the American ambassador at his place. One of our teammates, Dale DeBruin, was invited to go back that night to play the piano for the ambassador and his guests at dinner. What an experience for him.

We took a train from Finland to Italy, and that trip seemed as though it might last forever. We weren't in sleeper cars, so Reardon and I walked back to the sleeper car area and found a unit no one was using. A little later, a beautiful girl came in, no doubt wondering why we were there. We were polite to her, and when we thought she had gone to sleep, Mike and I talked about how attractive she was. Even if she was awake, we didn't figure it would matter; she didn't speak English. We didn't say anything too over the top, but if she understood us, she'd probably have told us to shut up, leave, or call for help... right?

About an hour later, the door opened. We looked up to find Eldon. He said, "Oh, I see you met my little interpreter friend."

Uh-oh! She *did* speak English!

We left the room for two reasons: the embarrassment we were sure we were dying from, and they were going to cut all the sleeper cars off at our next stop somewhere in Germany. That would have found us stranded, which obviously wouldn't have been good.

13

BEST SEASON EVER

My sophomore year was nothing short of magical for our team. We had just about everybody back from the year before and were overwhelming favorites to win the conference. Our team started the season with nineteen straight wins before losing at Toledo in probably our worst performance of the year. We couldn't shoot, play defense, rebound, or pass. Other than that, we played great.

After winning around the fifteenth straight game of the year, we finally broke into the national rankings before the Toledo loss. We rattled off three more wins before traveling to South Bend to take on the number eight team in the country, Notre Dame—again. Our All-Conference guard, Jeff Tyson, threw in a thirty-five-foot jump shot at the buzzer to send the game into overtime, and it was a thriller of a game.

The officials got the best of us. The other team's All-American forward, Adrian Dantley, went to the free-throw line *ten* times, and we lost in overtime. I think the officials even tried calling a foul on our manager at one point. It was that bad. Dantley became an All-Pro NBA performer, so I guess that game proved to everyone he could shoot free throws, and more importantly, that we were for real.

We had to shake off that loss in a hurry. We traveled to Miami of Ohio for what would be the game that determined the conference title. Our team played well and wound up winning by fifteen, and then we beat Bowling Green at home to put the exclamation point on things. That gave us the mid-American conference championship, and a guaranteed spot in the NCAA Tournament.

Not only was the Miami win a big one, but it was the site of one of those little "welcome to the team" moments. The night before the game, we went out to eat and then to a little ice cream shop on the streets of Oxford, Ohio. I happened to be last in line, and Griffin hung with me inside until I was done. We walked outside together, and Paul handed his cone to a teammate and grabbed me in what was called "the hook"—when someone puts their index fingers in the sides of your mouth and pulls your lips back, causing enough pain to make your eyes water.

Another guy grabbed my cone so that I wouldn't drop it. Such caring teammates, saving my ice cream and not me! The hook lasted for about fifteen seconds and cut my lip, soliciting laughter from my friends and nothing but agony from me. Once done, I said some choice words, and Griffin said, "Shut up, rookie." I knew then I would receive zero sympathy, but I also knew I was, without a doubt, one of them.

The celebration after the Bowling Green game was something else. In those days, Read Fieldhouse on campus held 10,800 people and was packed for most of our games. You'd find people sitting in aisles and on the floor near the court. That last game against Bowling Green was no exception, and I don't think anybody left until the celebration and trophy presentation was over.

The NCAA Tournament was next, and we drew Virginia Tech in the first game. Coincidently, that game was at Notre Dame, and we started rough, finding ourselves down ten points at halftime. The second half was a different story, even though our All-Tournament forward, Tom Cutter, got in foul trouble and had yours truly fill in for him until Coach Miller felt it was time to get him back in the game. We wound up coming back, tying the game in regulation and winning by ten in overtime.

Game Two in the tournament was in Baton Rouge, on the Louisiana State University campus. Our opponent was Marquette, ranked second in the nation behind Indiana, who went undefeated that year and won the NCAA Championship, and, to this day, is the last team to go undefeated. It was another great game, but we made some costly turnovers down the stretch and got beat 63-58.

The season was over, but what a season it was.

Our great success almost came tumbling down because of decisions made by nineteen- and twenty-year-old kids. Following a game played against Eastern Michigan in Ypsilanti, Michigan, Coach Miller gave us the option of going home since many of the players lived in that area, or riding back to campus with a friend or family member. Five of us decided to ride back with my roommate, Kevin, who had driven his car to watch the game. The first thing we did was to stop at a party store. Each of us bought a twelve-pack of beer—six twelve-packs for the hour and forty-five-minute drive home.

We were on Interstate 94, going home, and a snowstorm fell upon us. Suddenly, we saw flashing lights behind us. Uh-oh! Kevin pulled over while the rest of us began shoving beer under our seats. The problem was the guys in the back were pushing theirs forward and those of us in the front were pushing our twelve-packs back, causing a goat rodeo of idiocy.

An officer came to the window, saw the circus going on, and asked Kevin if he'd been drinking. He answered, yes; he'd had two beers. The officer asked him to step out of the car and walk a straight line. That turned out to be an issue. A semi-truck went by and the wind knocked Kevin right to the ground. We all laughed, but the situation was certainly no a laughing matter.

The officer told Kevin to get back in the car, take the next exit, and pull into the parking lot of a restaurant just off the exit. We took off and the police car followed us. The exit was about a half-mile away, so we got off, drove to an area with lights, and yelled, "This is it, turn!" just as soon as we spotted the restaurant.

Kevin yanked the wheel and went right into a snowbank. Stuck, we got out and tried to push the car out. One of the officers rolled down their window and screamed, "Tell the idiot to straighten out his wheels!"

Sure enough, we got out of the snow and into the parking lot. The officers escorted us into the restaurant, took Kevin's keys, gave them to the owner, and told him to pour as much coffee down our throats as possible for an hour. Only then could he give our keys back so we could drive home.

After about fifteen minutes, we were playing pool and having a party. The owner threw the keys at Kevin and said, "You guys get out of here and don't come back." So off we went into the snowstorm to drive home and find out where the parties were on campus that night. Stupid doesn't begin to describe our plight that night.

I worked at Ford Motor Company during my summer breaks after my second year at WMU, which allowed me to have some spending money in college. My dad knew lots of people in all aspects of the plant and was highly respected, just like in our community. I had a full-ride basketball scholarship, so school didn't have to be funded by me or my parents. Still, Dad got me those jobs with his connections, and working on the production line provided some excellent money and taught me a lot of lessons.

Ford Motor Company was fantastic to our family and my siblings, and I feel such a strong commitment to them. My brother also worked at Ford during the summer, as did my sister's husband, Tom. I worked hard labor on the assembly line while the two of them had the gravy job of working "security" at the front gates. I use that term, security, loosely—they didn't carry guns or do much else but sit in a little hut. They'll tell you they were imperative to the great success and protection of the company, but, nah.

I was supposed to produce a certain amount of product during my eight-hour shift. The bosses and union guys didn't want us going over that amount due to negotiations and also not making them look bad… Whatever that meant. I got good enough at my job that I'd get my production done in about four or five hours, which gave me enough time to duck out and get nine holes of golf in and then come back to punch my time card, or—not a very good thing—have someone punch out for me. I skipped my scheduled breaks and lunch so I could get that round of golf in.

To this day, I still remember how to do that job. I'd grab two u-joints that needed grinding down, put them in a grinding machine, push a button to have them rotate, put in two more the same way, and do that eight times before hitting two buttons. The machine finished grinding all of them down. When it was done with its grinding job, I did the same thing all over again, for eight hours a day. In my case, maybe four or five hours.

Academically, I once again did well. My GPA was about 3.5, but basketball was the priority. Kevin and I were both in the business school and decided we wanted to get our degrees in Business Education and become teachers and coaches. I loved working with younger kids each time I got to work the camps in the summer, and it was something I was passionate about and thought I did reasonably well with.

To come clean, I was going to college to play basketball. The school thing was a side job, but becoming a coach later on truly excited me.

14

THE YEAR AFTER

I found my first true love! That lasted a few months before she said *adios*, and I was heartbroken.

She knew she'd had the best and came crawling back. However, after a few months, she boogied again—heartbreak number two. Never fear! Again, she came back. Third time's a charm? Now, I may not have been a rocket scientist, but I thought better and said, "No thanks!"

Thank goodness. I wasn't aware of it at the time, but something else was in store for me.

When recruits came into town, we usually asked if they had any interest in going to a bar. If they said yes, we headed out to Coral Gables for Friday Happy Hour. You could get a pitcher for seventy-five cents, making for a cheap afternoon. Even with that, we still sometimes thought just having seventy-five cents was a luxury.

On one occasion, a big WMU booster walked into Coral Gables to handle some business on a night my friends and I just so happened to be there. We called over to him and he sat down, had a beer with us, and then asked how much the pitchers cost. When he heard how cheap they were, he called the waitress over and said, "We'll have a dozen pitchers."

We were awestruck. Not only that, but when we finished, he invited us over to his house and cooked us huge steaks, potatoes, and served us more beer. Luxury indeed!

I couldn't wait for our junior year to arrive. Following last year's season, I began trying to prepare myself for the upcoming year ahead of time. I wanted to be sure I made an impact, and I busted my buns in the off-season to make sure it happened.

I got up at 4:00 in the morning, ran, and then went to work at Ford. When I got home at night, I took another run, did a half-dozen drills, and I even took those rides from my childhood, bouncing a basketball while pedaling my bike. I found nights to play in a pickup game somewhere within forty-five minutes from home where better players than I were at.

Yep—I returned from Romeo that summer as a whole new player. I was back on campus and ready to play. The season started, and guess where I was? On the bench.

It wasn't because I wasn't playing well, but because the Wednesday ahead of Thanksgiving before practice even started, I went down on my knees and couldn't breathe. Come to find out, I suffered a collapsed lung. There was a hole about halfway down one of my lungs. I wasn't permitted to play in our first game of the year, and I was crushed. I was supposed to be the starting post player, along with Tom Cutter.

I complained more to doctors, trainers, and coaches than anyone in history, but to no avail. I cried myself dry all the way home to Romeo the night it happened. They finally let me out of the hospital while I had that hole in my lung so that I could make the three-hour drive home for Thanksgiving.

Even though I had to sit out our first game, I started the next game. We won, starting 2 and 0 in the year, and we were pretty darn excited. I can't remember the exact numbers, but I scored many points and got a lot of rebounds. Pumped would be an understatement for how my emotions and feelings were, and my confidence was at an all-time high. We played Michigan State in East Lansing the next game and wound up beating them as well, 3-

0, thanks to a late-game charge that my roommate, Mike Reardon, took against a guy that had a body like a semi-truck.

I won't go on rattling off all highlights, but we lost two games before the new year started. Those losses were to second-ranked Marquette, coached by the legendary Al McGuire, and to fourth-ranked the University of Alabama by nine points. The season was starting as I'd hoped it would, heading into the Mid-American portion of the schedule once January came.

We got two conference wins quickly, but it seemed like things weren't progressing as they should. The season unraveled toward the end. At one point, we lost seven games in a row, finishing our season 14 and 13. Some bizarre things happened that year, but I'm a part of it since I was on the team. It ended roughly, but it was a winning season, and I looked toward my senior season, ready to take another step forward.

ENDING THE CAREER

My senior season was filled with great anticipation. Little did I know it would be my most disappointing and frustrating school year ever. I was the starting center, and we started with a nice win over Valparaiso University, where I played a great game.

Two of our losses before Christmas were a close game to second-ranked Marquette and top-ten Michigan State, who had a dude named Magic Johnson. He made it to the Final Four of the NCAA tournament that year. That put us at 3 and 4 at Christmas, which also included a loss to the first-ranked team in Division 2, Grand Valley State. Not a great start, but not horrible either. We were eager to get to the conference portion of the season.

Even with that record, we were anxious to start league play. However, our coach, Dick Shilts, had a team meeting and told us that if we were going to continue losing, we would lose with younger players on the court. Keep in mind that Dick Shilts is one of the finest people I've ever known, and we're still friends to this day. But that meeting burst the bubble of several of us, and the team chemistry went in the tank.

That was his decision, and a decision he truly believed was right for his program. We played, but it was sparingly. We finished the season 7 and 20, and it was a very long season. There was more than one night that I went home, laid in my bed, and cried; knowing my basketball days were ending in such a negative and disappointing way. I was ready to be done playing, and my enjoyment for the game I'd played since I was five was gone.

One positive point came toward the end of that year. At our last practice, the juniors and seniors played the freshmen and sophomores in a scrimmage. Us upperclassmen wound up beating the freshmen and sophomores by about thirty or forty points. It was an excellent way to end things, and it gave us older guys a little satisfaction.

The team chemistry wasn't good; there wasn't anyone in the younger group who was a solid leader, and our role as seniors was not what it could have been. In addition, I allowed my schoolwork to become affected. That was my fault—not that of Dick Shilts, a teammate, or a girl. There was nobody to blame but me.

My motivation during the season waned, and I wish I would have done a better job of being a contributing teammate. Despite everything, I was still the leading rebounder. That train has left the station, and there is zero I can do about it now. The season was over, and it was time to move on to a new chapter of my life. With all the frustration, there were good things that year that helped make my time in college a success.

Playing a Division 1 sport in college has always meant so much to me. Those are the years that I believe were the most exciting and influential of my life. Bonding with a group of people that became your best friends and which you did everything with is something you can't imagine unless you've done it. To this day, I'm in almost daily contact with many of them through technology.

Team practices were excruciating at times, but those are the times I'd give almost anything to go through again. Saturday afternoon games in Read Fieldhouse in front of a packed crowd—which was the only show in town, and a good one at that—running on the floor before games; hearing your name announced over the speakers at the start of each game; and competing at that level was exhilarating.

I can't thank every coach I've ever had enough for what they've done for me, and I've made it abundantly clear to all of them how much they mean to me: Jim Feldkamp, Jerry Barr, Eldon Miller, Dick Shilts. Unfortunately, with a few things, mainly basketball, that were going on, my academic interests were almost nil. I put little effort into my classes and suffered the results I deserved. However, I always knew where I stood on the way toward graduation.

There were many lessons and experiences during my WMU days. One thing I've discovered is that kids today have more things to do at home than were imaginable during that time. What did we do back then? Went out! And did we ever go out. Finding us at home was a rarity. We were always looking for action, where lots of people would be. I wouldn't trade it for anything.

But, it was time for big boy life.

I wasn't as nervous as I was confused and anxious about finding a steady job and paying bills. What did I have going for me now that basketball was over with, and how would I live without it? If you do something nearly all the time for fifteen to twenty years, and then you don't do it any longer when you're only twenty-two years old, it hits you funny, and not haha-funny. At least it did me. My last school year wasn't a fun period of my life, from the second half of my junior year through the end of the first semester of the final year.

I'd loved school from the time I was in kindergarten until I graduated college because sports were essential to me, and I always played them. Heck, there were times in high school that I asked to go to the restroom and then headed to the gym to shoot around. I don't know if my teachers knew I was doing that, but it worked... except for the times Principal Dave Olson or Assistant Principal John Allen saw me go in. The first time, I told them I was on the way to the bathroom. That happened a few times, but they were smart guys, and when they saw me out of class later on, they laughed and said, "Get back to class, and no, you're not going to shoot baskets."

No problem. Who in their right mind would want those two

hollering or getting mad at you? They were terrific men to have in charge. The school was in great hands with them.

Working on my Bachelor's degree at Western wasn't much better. I knew that basketball was why I was going to college, free of charge. Well, not totally free—we had to pay a fifty-cent "social fee" each semester. I'm sure that was for the keg parties taking place at the end of our dorm hallway. I wasn't committed to that academic thing and didn't work all that hard at it as I should have.

Again, I did okay at the beginning, but then I just kind of skated along. Today, I can't read enough *true* information that I find through different sources. I want to know information, and like many others, if I could do it over again, I'd…

Fortunately, I was able to do my student teaching at Vicksburg High School, where I had an amazing experience teaching business with Frank Holmes. There were great people to work with, and the basketball coach, Paul Gorsuch, allowed me to help him coach.

My responsibilities were limited, but at least I got involved with hoops again, and I really couldn't have asked for a better opportunity than the one I had there. It renewed my desire to do an excellent job at something as I'd previously done with basketball. The school didn't have a great basketball history, but Paul was an outstanding coach and led the team to the conference championship, which many thought wasn't possible. Expectations weren't high for the team, but we tried to keep the scores in the thirties, and that seemed to work.

Once I was done with my student teaching, I went home to Romeo. It was time to try and find a big boy job in education. Sending out resumes, calling to find interviews, and then going through those interviews was nerve-racking. I was starting real life without the benefit of mooching off my parents or living and going to college for free.

I had had a great first three years of college, except for the fact that a girl made my life miserable, but I know that I'm not the first person to experience that one. It passed and wasn't on my radar as much, and I'm thrilled that relationship didn't work out—my life today would not have been the same. It was the last year of basketball and the year following it that had me kind of depressed about my next steps. It was hard to believe that any other experience could possibly match my life with basketball.

Ha! It's comical now, isn't it? You and I know that life has so many incredible—both good and bad—experiences we can't imagine when we're in our early twenties.

STARTING MY BIG BOY LIFE

Bill Johnston, the principal at Mattawan High School, called me when I was home in Romeo and asked me to interview for an opening they had for a teacher. He was one of the top two principals I had in my career, along with Athletic Director Rich Ames and Superintendent Jim Weeldreyer.

What was a small school with about 450 students is now a school with close to 1,500 students. They've done an excellent job in marketing their school and having good people on board.

I never applied, but I think Bill got my name through Western and probably knew I was a player there. His loyalty to WMU is far-reaching, as is his passion and knowledge for sports. In his post-education career, he became the chair of Western's board.

The interview went well. I was offered the job and accepted it. I was on my way! That was the beginning of a tremendous four years.

My salary that first year of teaching was $10,400. I had a paycheck to start paying bills: car payment, rent for my apartment that I shared with a couple of other guys, food, and gas for the car. That's about all I could afford, as $10,400 sure didn't go far. It wasn't considered a significant amount of money, even in 1980.

Thinking about making that amount now and having to live on

it... Well, that's a scary thought, right? The truth is that when teachers first start out, they make about that much money—comparatively speaking, with inflation and the general costs of living.

When you seriously think about it, it's incredible that we expect kids to go into the education field and *know* that when they graduate, their annual pay will be around $30,000 to $35,000 and that they'll never make six figures. Attracting the brightest minds sure isn't going to happen that way, and the salary progression throughout a career of, say, thirty-five years doesn't get too high either. I'm out of that field today, so I don't have a say in these things, but it's accurate nonetheless.

Our government's money expenditures on things you can't imagine and not paying teachers the wages they should be paid is mind-boggling. Some have said that social programs don't spend as much as people think, but when you see several different kinds of social aid in all departments, there should be some adjustments made. It's not enough to throw money at the schools, but with the advancements in technology, there is so much money that would be saved by not building $100-million schools and running them in the traditional manner.

I'll stop my tangent on the issue, but lots of waste will continue if we don't roll with the times.

I also coached football and basketball at Mattawan, which gave me another $700 to $800, but I volunteered as a varsity basketball assistant for Ed Staron since his coaching staff was already in place.

Ed—Doc, as we called him—was full of fire and passionate with his coaching. He was a great person to learn from, and I volunteered for all four years and never thought anything about it in terms of not being paid. One of the issues in today's high school sports is that most young kids who go into coaching, and many other professions, don't want to volunteer when they first start out. Say what you want, but it is the truth.

In my first year, I had to prepare for four different classes, plus football and basketball coaching, which made me not so great of a teacher. I wanted to be a wonderful teacher, but I had too much on my plate to be effective at all of it. I spent almost every waking minute trying to prepare, and I'm glad that I was young enough to have the energy for it and not get burned out. However, there never seemed to be enough time.

Principal Bill Johnston and I got to be terrific friends with about six other people on the staff. We socialized together and did the "work hard, play hard" thing. When we were at school, the staff and I were all business, and we never took advantage of our relationship with him. We had too much respect for him and the job he did.

Around April, Bill called me into his office. Going into his office wasn't a big deal, so I wasn't overly concerned. But in that meeting, he told me my teaching was lacking and I needed to get much better at what I was doing. Holy smokes! I wasn't expecting that, and it certainly wasn't something I wanted to hear. Bill explained that if I couldn't improve, other steps would have to occur. For the next twenty-four hours, I was angry and hurt. Those feelings were a result of my competitive nature and background.

That meeting took place the day before Spring Break, so I had some time to settle down. I realized I'd better take his recommendations and get cooking. That discussion ended up being one of the best ones I've ever had with a superior in my thirty-eight years in education. He was there to help and not just reprimand as some others do. He realized I needed help and allowed me to improve, and he gave me suggestions on how to do so. It was like many other challenging discussions where things need to be said but might offend someone if they can't handle the truth.

My athletics background undoubtedly helped me; coaches reprimanded me in the past and I hated it at the time but appreciated it later. I imagine how things would be if those coaches would not have corrected me and continued to allow me to make the same mistakes.

In the long run, those who take suggestions to heart are the beneficiaries and appreciate what's happened to make things better. It does, indeed, initially hurt, but over time, it helps if you can sit back and try to make life better for everyone involved. I have no doubt that correlates to young kids who want to be the president of a company when they graduate. Many don't want to work to get better at what they do, make the necessary mistakes, or learn the lessons required to one day become a president that understands how successful businesses are run. It comes back around to many parents telling their children that they deserve the best instead of working for it.

When our generation was younger and we gave the teacher or coach some lip service, we got called in—along with our parents—for reprimand, and our parents were totally on the side of the teacher or coach. Do you remember dreading going home, fearing the wrath of your parents?

Nowadays, the mentality of parental support has decreased significantly. Teachers hear, "Don't say that to my child. You're mistaken. It would be best if you never criticized him. Always encourage and give praise." In sports, it's, "Coach, you need to play my little Bobby because he's the best you have. I don't care if he's shooting 10% from the floor. Play him over Joey, who's shooting 60% from the floor anyway."

As do most professionals, I believe that this mentality, sense of entitlement, and lack of discipline come from the enormous increase in youth sports. Parents who have their kids playing on travel teams in different sports at a young age think that their kids are entitled to play when they get older because they've invested time and money. I've gone through youth sports opportunities with my kids and experienced them. One time, I even became one of "those" parents and did something stupid, but I was fortunate enough that the coach continued to treat me nicely. Regardless, I was embarrassed after what I'd done and knew I wouldn't do it again.

It's kind of funny when dads are their kids' coaches. In baseball, the coach's son is almost always the pitcher and shortstop. In basketball, they're the point guard, no matter their size, and always have to be the one who shoots the most. In football, the coach's son, in most cases, is the quarterback. Those parents are usually great people and wonderful parents. However, emotions come out, many times with claws and fangs.

I wonder how many times a great chemistry teacher, maybe the best in the country, has 2,500 people come and watch them present the most distinguished lecture of the school that year. More than likely none, but win a big game or two in athletics for your school, and you have mobs of people coming to watch the rest of the games, as it's almost never questioned that athletics is not only the most visible part of a school but also its most emotional.

17

MARGARET JOANNA EWALD

During my college years, my closest friends were Kevin McSkimming and Mike Reardon. Usually, whatever one did, the other two did as well. We had a lot in common, loved being around one another, and the relationships we were building between the three of us were a great fit.

Each of us came from family backgrounds rooted in goodness and love and not excellent financial means. During the summers away from school, we always kept in contact. Kevin lived about forty-five minutes away from me, but Mike lived in Fremont, Ohio, about three hours away. One summer, my dad got Mike a job at Ford Motor and he lived with my family. That was the type of closeness the three of us had.

It was always interesting when one of us started dating. Relationships weren't meant to last; the other two were unmercifully tough on the guy with the girl. Heaven forbid anything disrupt the relationship between the three of us. Thus, nobody had a girlfriend that lasted long during those college years, which was okay. Having fun with the boys always seemed more fun... even though girls had that spell that only they possess.

After we graduated, I began my teaching career. Kevin moved

back to the Detroit area, and Mike started his Master's program at Western. Kevin started working for the Bic Corporation, I was living on my own, and Mike lived with his parents while he finished his degree. It seemed as though we were growing up, and the three of us could start a relationship with a girl since the other two weren't around as much to dish out the routine abuse.

Mike started dating, and it turned out she was lovely and very attractive. She was completing her senior year at Western, and since Mike lived in town, he and I saw each other often; not every day but probably four or five days a week. However, I was wrapped up in my teaching career and busy trying to excel. On occasional weekends, Mike and his girlfriend came over or we met at a party or another friend's place. Pretty soon, it seemed the three of us were friends and Kevin was out of the circle because he wasn't in town. We missed Kevin, which was something we both had to adjust to.

One night, Mike had a party at his folks' house, and several of our friends were there. I was going on a road trip with some of my colleagues from Mattawan early the next day to watch Western Michigan play football at Ball State, so I knew I had to leave early. When I said I was headed home, Mike started the "You're a wimp for leaving early" grief that had been part of our commonplace joking for the last five years.

Mike's girlfriend, who fit right into our group, started in on me as well. But, as we moved away from Mike, she said she didn't think I should leave, and she didn't want me to go. I responded by saying I didn't want to leave, that hanging out with them was always fun. She answered that it was always hard for her when I left.

Uh-oh. With that, I was out the door, but knew there could be trouble on the horizon.

Within twenty-four hours, I found out she had broken up with Mike. I was apprehensive about things, especially when she came to my apartment soon after. I was afraid of what was happening, but within a day or two, we were dating. Mike didn't know, but it was only a matter of time before he found out, and that would undoubtedly cause a significant problem with our friendship, which I had to prepare for.

Should I date her or not? I could very well lose my best friend over a girl.

We told him, and he was obviously mad. I didn't blame him one bit. Some of our friends were also ticked at me, and so my decision to date her was one I knew had to be a serious commitment. She knew that as well. So, she and I hung out a ton during the next two weeks, and then I asked Peg Ewald to marry me. Two weeks! I knew if I was going to give up my best friend for her, it better be forever.

We had known each other for the months she was dating Mike, and during that time, she had become a great friend. Peg had qualities I admired and worshiped. And so, on July 25, 1981, Peg and I were married in Cadillac, Michigan, and have been married ever since.

That's right. Two weeks of dating, a proposal, and a marriage. Peg has been my rock and the mother of our four children while doing things in her life that should qualify her to be a real American hero. I'm not sure how I was so blessed with her. I definitely took a step up when we married.

It took Mike and me five years to talk again, but he reached out to me, and even though it's still on both of our minds, we've worked through things and are friends again.

Mike married a woman I introduced him to. She lived behind my house back in Romeo. I always thought she was a tad different. They divorced after thirty years, but he has since gotten married again to a delightful woman. I'm more than just a little happy for him. We still contact each other at least a couple of times a week.

Our time in Mattawan ended with Peg and me taking the seniors on a class trip to Orlando, Florida, along with Bill Johnston and his wife, Ronda Stryker. The plan was to get a chartered bus and make the trip down, which would take about twenty-four hours based on the stops we'd have to make and the prime-time Florida traffic that would no doubt be present.

There was a slight wrinkle in the trip. Peg and Ronda were pregnant, both with their first child. They had it tough, but my wife was eight months pregnant, while Ronda was six months along. When we arrived in Florida, Peg's ankles were so swollen that she had to stay in bed for almost twenty-four hours to get the swelling and pain out while I enjoyed the lovely hotel pool and made sure the kids were under control.

We did the normal Disney things like going to the different theme parks, but after a couple of days of walking around, the ankle thing popped up again, and Peg couldn't make the trip to the Wet n' Wild water park that we had planned. She stayed back, and the rest of us went.

I had quite a bit of fun as a twenty-six-year-old guy lying in the sun, which turned out to be a major mistake. The sunburn I got was almost unbearable. The trip back to Michigan was more than just a little tricky. Peg's pregnancy was an issue for her and my sunburn hurt like crazy.

Once it was time to get a better job, having to say goodbye to my colleagues at Mattawan and my closest friends was tough. The funny thing is that where I was eventually going was only eight miles away, but it seems like you don't have the contact with people you once did when you're working.

18

RESPONSIBILITIES ARE INCREASING

Our first child came on June 20, 1983. Marc Donald Throop was an incredible gift for us.

Like most parents when they have their first child, life changes dramatically. The days of going out with the boys, along with Peg and I simply doing what we wanted, were over. The fact we had no money also played a large part in hunkering down a lot more.

I'm not sure how I can explain, although most parents feel the same way, how much I loved that kid and still do to this day. He graduated from Gull Lake with around a 3.0 GPA and then took a few years to figure out what the heck he was going to do. Although he went to college, it just wasn't his bag, and I supported that.

He was great with his hands and had a knack for fixing and making things. Peg was an Industrial Marketing major in college, so I'm sure he got that from her. Today, Marc is a journeyman fabricator sheet metal worker, and the things he can do and make are nothing short of a miracle in my eyes. He's also got a family—which means I have grandkids to spoil—and they are a blessing to us.

Marc is a tremendous dad! I am so proud of that kid for what he's accomplished and the father he is that I often have to stop myself from crying. We were happy they lived near us; it meant we got to have their kids over often. Natalie spent the night once a week. Their other daughter, Annalise (Annie), is from a previous relationship that Marc's wife Lyndsie had, and so Annie goes to her biological dad's on the weekend. It's an amicable relationship between all of them, which makes things suitable for Annie. Later, MerryJane was born, which gave us three granddaughters.

For Peg and me, Child Number Two came along on June 20, 1986. When Kelli Regina Throop was born, we looked at her and said, "Oh, that poor girl. She has to grow up looking like that!" She wasn't pretty at first, but that was because the umbilical cord had wrapped around her neck during birth. It didn't take long for all that to change. She was a gorgeous kid.

Kelli played basketball and volleyball in high school and was an All-Conference player. She graduated from Western Michigan University and then took a job in Chicago, where she worked in the logistics world. It was an outstanding job, but her boyfriend was back in Gull Lake. She wasn't coming back until there was a commitment from him for the long term, even though they'd dated for nine years, which we joke about often considering mine and Peg's whirlwind romance.

When Trevor Miller proposed to Kelli, she went to her boss two days later and gave him her two-week notice. I think she worked longer than that, but she wound up coming home, and now she and Trevor live on Gull Lake. We love Trevor and think he's perfect for her.

On September 24, 1993, Joshua William Throop was born. My son Marc was in the delivery room with me when Josh was born, and that was an excellent experience for me and Marc. At the time, we were great friends with Jeff and Donna Mitchell, and Marc was staying at their house while Peg and I journeyed to the hospital. Once we were close to birthing time, we called Donna and told her to bring Marc, so she was in the room also.

When the nurse put Josh on the scale and he was listed at ten pounds, one ounce, we yelled, "A ten-pounder!" Growing up, he was mild-mannered when he was at home, and like our other kids, he got involved in sports. He was a good baseball and basketball player, and he too was an All-Conference player.

Josh could have continued his athletic career; some small schools showed interest in his baseball skills, but he was determined to go to a school for his academic priorities. He chose the University of Alabama, where he had a two-thirds scholarship due to his academic achievements in high school. He graduated in three and a half years. Josh went on to receive his Masters from the University of Georgia in Athens in Accounting, and before he even started that program, he was offered a job with the accounting firm of Ernst and Young in Atlanta, and had a position waiting for him upon his graduation.

While Josh was at the University of Alabama, he met his wife. Morgan Miller is as sweet as they come. Originally from Suwanee, Georgia, she now owns a store in Athens, Georgia called The Indigo Child. If you're ever in the area, stop in and buy something! I call it a high-end hippy store, but they've got things young girls desire.

Finally, on September 28, 1998, Noah William Throop was born. We took Kelli into the delivery room for his birth, but she wasn't overly enamored with the process, so we had her sit outside of the room when delivery started. Although Noah was unexpected, he has been nothing short of a blessing, even with the fifteen-year age difference between him and Marc, our oldest.

Wait... None of our children were expected. Blessings nonetheless!

We thought the elementary school would name their suspension room after Noah because he spent so many of his early days there. He was highly active and full of life. Noah liked sports but wasn't big into working at them. He wanted to keep up with teams but just didn't have the passion for getting involved at an early age, which later changed.

When Noah was a sophomore in high school, he started working hard at his basketball and baseball skills. I think he's worked harder than any of the other kids at athletics, and he saw the fruits of his labor through his success. Upon high school graduation, Noah also decided to attend Alabama, which we were pleased about, as we had fallen in love with UA.

19

COACHING

I stayed at Mattawan for four wonderful years. My first teaching and coaching jobs, meeting great people, and having outstanding students—some of which I've continued to be friends with today—made that season of my life a wonderful time. Making great friends during that time is something I'll never forget, and my growth as an educator was more than I could have imagined. Bill Johnston, Rich Ames, Ed Staron, and many others helped with that process.

Bill was a premier principal, and I learned a boatload from him. Ed was a darn intense coach but knew what the heck he was doing, and Rich always was an ear I could speak to. Even thinking about leaving that school was tough to imagine. However, I wanted to be a head varsity basketball coach somewhere, and I also wanted to make a difference in kids' lives in that role.

I always thought I'd coach at the collegiate level, but when my children started coming, I didn't want to be gone from the house overnight. While working a camp one summer, a coach from a Division 1 school and I hit it off well. He told me that they had an opening, and we discussed it briefly. One of the first things he told me was that I'd probably be gone from home close to 250 nights a year. My interest quickly subsided. I was scared of being away from my family that often.

In the spring of 1983, I received a call from a guy named Stu Ellens, the principal at Paw Paw High School. He wanted to know if I'd be interested in interviewing for the Varsity Basketball Coach and Business Teacher positions. Seeing that they were positions I wanted to be in, I got my application materials ready and went to a little place called Tea Pot Dome and met Stu for breakfast. That restaurant was about the size of a decent-sized bedroom. The half-dozen tables inside were packed with people eating breakfast. Privacy was undoubtedly not going to happen, and, as I learned later, that was Stu's deliberate intent. They knew what we were doing there. The interview went well, and a couple of days later, I was offered the job and accepted.

My first year coaching in Paw Paw was difficult in regards to the basketball team. We had a player, the best returning player from the year prior, who was a little on the rebellious side. Nice kid, but "confident."

Back then, one of my rules was that players could not wear T-shirts depicting alcohol. Kicked off the team for it? No way, but the offense carried a small consequence. Though the trend was just beginning and hadn't yet been prohibited by the school—or just about any school, for that matter—it has since been disallowed in most districts.

In addition to breaking my "no alcohol shirt" rule, the player had also gotten into some big trouble for its time. I had to talk with him about it and let him know that there would be consequences for those actions, as well, but, without question, he deserved another chance, as that's what we all deserve in most cases. I also let him know he had the opportunity to either accept his consequences or decide not to be a part of the team.

The next day, he came to school wearing an alcohol-related shirt, and when I saw him, I asked if we needed to talk again. He said, "Not really," so that was the end of it... until his lawyer called to tell me I was making a big mistake by giving him consequences when the kid's trial had not yet occurred. When I told him the boy admitted to me that he had done what was alleged to have happened, the attorney said, "Well, I guess he shouldn't have told you." That attorney and I got to be friends later on, and I have a great deal of respect for the job he later did as a judge.

Our first year in Paw Paw was tough, to say the least. We wound up going 1 and 20 as a final record on the season, but our team consisted of some good players, like seniors that included Joel Patterson, Dave Mastenbrook, Frank Quantz, Bob Humphries, and Todd Conklin. The second year, we won two games instead of just one—a 100% improvement from the previous year!

Many people were beginning to wonder why I was hired. However, we laid incredible amounts of groundwork during that time, and kids were coming through the program that were making a difference. Due to the poor record of my first two seasons, a petition was presented, signed by about 200 people, to have me removed from my job as the coach. *200 people!* That bothered me a great deal until I saw that it had signatures from people living in different parts of the country—friends and family members of the person who started the petition—and then it was simply something to laugh about.

In year three, we turned the corner, still only going 11 and 10 on the season, but people were getting more excited, especially knowing what we had coming back the following year. But, that next year was one of peaks and valleys. Regardless, we won the conference championship, finished the season with an excellent record, were named the number-one team in Southwestern Lower Michigan, and ranked in the top five in the state. I was named the Regional Coach of the Year and second for Michigan's Coach of the Year.

That should have made things feel great, but our locker room wasn't very cohesive. Individuals' accomplishments began taking priority over what was best for the team. In most cases, those kinds of feelings are bred at home and by those who do not have the best interest of the kid or the team. I believe we would have been a team that could have done so much better if it weren't for that fact.

However, as a coach, I have to take responsibility as well. I was supposed to build that cohesiveness. Even with the team's

89

accomplishments, we lost in the district tournament game, ending the year. It was kind of a relief because it was such a difficult team to get to play together, and some personalities were tough to handle. Despite some of those difficulties, I would still do anything I could to help those kids today.

The following year was one of the best seasons I've ever had due to the kids on the team. One of those returning players told me, "We aren't going to let what happened last year happen this year." We had an outstanding record, once again ranked in the top five in the state at one point, and we had players and parents that made coaching a ton of fun. We didn't win the championship, but it was a season full of success and wonderful times.

Despite that year being one of the best I'd ever have, it was time to leave Paw Paw for reasons that were by no means major. Something told Peg and me that we needed to look around. I had no specific idea why, but those reasons would later become clear.

Peg and I had several amazing years getting to know the beautiful people of Paw Paw, and my growth there in my first experience as a head varsity basketball coach was enormous. It came with errors, but in life, you'll never learn anything unless you make mistakes to let you know how to do things right.

Paw Paw was the typical all-American town with a Main Street, shops, some bars, restaurants, and a general feel-good atmosphere. Peg and I enjoyed living there and being a part of their community. I grew to be terrific friends with people like Bob Johnson, Tom Baney, and Gary Kruizenga, to name a few.

Those guys stick out in my mind, as they were almost perfect about being honest with me in an encouraging way, especially in regards to how they thought my basketball teams might do better. My friends didn't hold against me what I did or did not do. We shook off our differences and would then go grab a beer. That's why they were such good friends. I also had their kids as players and students, and they were all fantastic kids.

A couple of others claimed to be my friends, but the second something didn't go right for their child, they turned on me like a corkscrew. I learned from those people also, and I am appreciative that things happened the way they did.

I've said that the best coaching job in the world is one at the orphanage. I once said that in an interview in the late 1980s and was told by my athletic director that it probably wasn't the smartest thing for me to say. It wasn't the first or last time I said something stupid.

NEW CHALLENGES

I n the spring of 1987, I received a phone call from Mike Foster, the Gull Lake High School Athletic Director. Gull Lake was generally a well-respected school. Again, I have no idea why, but Peg and I somehow knew what we had done at Paw Paw was good and that it was time to move on.

Leaving Paw Paw was extremely difficult. We were happy there and had made many friends. If you live in Paw Paw, don't move. You've got a good thing. However, we needed a change. Little did I know we'd find out why we'd left a few years later.

Mike and I met at a McDonald's halfway between the two schools. We sat and talked for quite a while, and then he said he wanted me to apply for the basketball coaching position based on our talk, what I'd done in Paw Paw, and what he'd heard from others. I should have given him the names and numbers of those that might not have been so gracious with their opinions.

Seriously, every coach, A.D., principal, and teacher has people who don't like them because they deal with their children. It's the nature of the business, and I get it.

I took Mike up on his offer to interview for the job. My initial interview was with Mike, Principal Bob Sickles, Assistant

Superintendent Chuck Roy, and Superintendent of Schools Tom Ryan. The interview went extremely well, and I was as relaxed as any interview I'd ever had for a couple of different reasons. First, on the way to the interview, I cranked up a tape of Bob Seger that got me juiced. The other reason was that I knew I had an interview at Forest Hills Central in the Grand Rapids area two days later, which was the job I thought I wanted.

Forest Hills Central was a Class A school. There were many great things happening there, including exceptional facilities and a positive reputation. The FHC interview went well, but something was missing and didn't feel right. The teaching position didn't jive with what I was looking for in my area.

The day after the FHC interview, Mike Foster called and offered me the position at Gull Lake. They knew I had interviewed at FHC. Mike said he needed to know by the next day whether I would accept. They'd discussed how to make a teaching position open up for me in the business department, and because of the timing, it all needed to happen quickly.

I called Forest Hills and asked them how things were progressing. The A.D. there was a man named Bob Rowbotham, who was a fantastic guy and had an outstanding reputation around the state as a top-notch A.D. He told me the teaching portion had become difficult to secure, but what they could initially offer was two hours in the classroom, and then I'd work the rest of the day as an in-school suspension supervisor. That wasn't very exciting to hear, although he said I'd be in a classroom full-time by year two.

I hung up with Bob, went home, and Peg and I discussed things. The next day, I knew I had to decide. Mike Foster called that morning, but I didn't take his call. I knew what he wanted. He called again shortly after lunch. I avoided him a second time and called Peg to ask her to come up to the school so we could talk some more.

In the meantime, Forest Hills also called and wanted me to take the position they'd offered. However, the teaching issue had not changed, so I told him how much I appreciated the interest, but I couldn't accept. He understood completely.

With that, I called Mike at Gull Lake and told him I'd take the job. Mike was elated and asked if we could meet later. I made the forty-minute drive that afternoon to finalize things. I got to talk again with what would be my first—and best ever—people in the principal and superintendent roles at Gull Lake.

They were excited to have me accept, and then, in these words, said, "Oh, by the way, can you teach computer classes?"

Dumbfounded was an understatement. Nevertheless, I immediately said, "Sure, no problem."

I was used to teaching accounting, marketing, and typing. Remember, computers weren't very popular back in 1987, but I knew I could figure it out. After all, I figured I had the entire summer to get ready. Uh-huh… right.

I took a computer home, and it took me three days to even learn how to turn it on and have something show up on the screen. I was frustrated and nervous, and I didn't think things would go well once I tried to teach kids. Sure, I could show them how to be frustrated, but teach them how to work a computer? *Maybe I can change the name of the class, and nobody will figure it out. Hmm…* I thought. Yeah, that probably wouldn't have worked out.

Finally, I got the thing working, and from then on, operating it was easy. The old Apple IIe machine was something I thought was as sophisticated and detailed as any computer could ever be. I went to conferences, read books on the new computer fad that was upon us, talked with college professors, and soaked up any other resource I could get my hands on that offered up knowledge to help me better educate.

As we've seen through the years, times have changed. Today, I think many of us *expect* kids to know more about that type of stuff by the time they start kindergarten than we even know at my age. You can call me crazy, but I think the person who helps deliver a child has been provided top-secret clearance on giving every baby born a technology gene or a chip implant through the help of aliens. Seriously, I saw that on the Internet and spent quite a bit of time repeatedly reading that same source. Told ya you could call me crazy.

I wanted to make a statement during my first meeting with the guys who would be part of the Gull Lake basketball team hopefuls. They walked in, but one kid had a hat on. In my opening remarks, I told him if he wanted to keep that hat on, he could, but to make sure he didn't let the door hit him on the butt on his way out.

Mike Foster was in the meeting and probably shivered, wondering, *What's he doing? Why the heck did I hire this guy?* As with just about everything, Mike walked hand in hand with me the entire way during the time he was my boss. A better A.D. you couldn't find anywhere.

We went to team camp that summer, so I didn't have much time with the guys before we left. Without question, the best player in the group was a handful... again! I had all the makings for how I'd started in Paw Paw with an excellent player who might not want to head in the same direction the rest of the team was going.

He didn't like how I talked to him or what I had to say at camp, so he walked out of the gym. I figured he was off to get a drink of water, even though it was taking a long time for him to return. Come to find out, when he walked out of the gym, he never came back to camp. He called his girlfriend to pick him up, and he left. I knew then that it was going to be a long year with that kid.

Funny thing, he wasn't at all a bad kid. Most of the students at school liked him, but everyone knew he was temperamental. He will always be one of those kids I'll look back on and say, "I wish I would have worked with him more."

When the season came around that first year, our favorite player showed up, stayed for most of the first practice, and then decided he wouldn't play. It was no doubt because of the conflict he and I were having, but it was his choice to leave. Two days later, he apologized and asked to come back. I so badly wanted to say yes, but would that do him, me, and the team any good? Based on what had happened during our early experiences, I was more than a little hesitant to let him return, but I wanted to nonetheless.

I called the guys into practice the next day and explained the scenario. I asked each of them to write down a YES or NO on a slip of paper based on whether they felt he should be allowed to return. There were thirteen guys on the team, so I knew we wouldn't have a tie. I also told them that the vote would not make the decision for me, as the responsibility of the decision was mine to make, but it would give me some much-needed insight

I opened up the first twelve ballots: six YES and six NO. The last one I opened said UNDECIDED. Are you kidding me? I laughed, but decided not to let the player back on the team. Even though we were losing our best player, based on our past interaction and his previous years, I knew not having him there would be in the team's best interest. As it turned out, he became a cheerleader on the cheer team that year.

On my first day of teaching at Gull Lake, I believed I'd made a mistake in leaving Paw Paw. I was homesick. However, the people in Gull Lake were nice to me, and I still remember my first day teaching keyboarding... Yes, keyboarding on electric typewriters.

There was a girl who sat in the first row, Lisa Piotrowicz. She seemed to have a carefree personality that made things better for me. Lisa was part of a group of five or six boys and girls that helped my transition without them even knowing. Lisa later became a varsity soccer coach at another school, but I lost track of her over the years. Fortunately, Facebook helped us reconnect. It's always fun to hear from and see former students and players. I'm willing to bet that most coaches and teachers feel that way.

Gull Lake was a place where there were probably a tad more vocal people than the norm, but I have great respect for most that I came into contact with. Most parents don't believe their kids are owed anything, but every parent loves their child. That's the difference. It was still a minimal number, but enough to make things miserable at times.

As Mike later told me, Gull Lake had many chiefs and not nearly enough warriors. Most were good—no, *outstanding*—people, but some were tough to deal with at times. In a recent New York study, over 80% of coaches said that parents are more challenging to deal with today than they used to be, and 60% of coaches said that they have had to consistently speak with parents about their poor behavior. It would be ideal to have all coaches say that those confrontations don't happen to them, but we can't.

In addition, coaches are more afraid to do something nowadays because some of them are afraid of causing unnecessary issues. Stuart Scott, the former ESPN announcer who passed away from cancer, once said, "Parents are the best thing about youth sports, but they are also the worst thing about youth sports." Families like the Uggens, Algers, Fuzacks, and Worgess, to name a few, knew the purpose of high school sports and the value of lessons learned from their children's involvement. Even though they probably didn't agree with every decision, they let us do our jobs and allowed their kids to gain valuable life experiences. They were active in the school but in a positive way and were there to help.

Again, the first few years at Gull Lake were tough from a win/loss standpoint, just as they had been in Paw Paw. We did many things to lay groundwork, but people weren't necessarily as patient as they were in Paw Paw. That old "chief/warrior" correlation no doubt was holding up progress. If not for kids like Derek Fleck, I may have gone crazy.

Derek would often calm me down, tell me things were going fine, and that eventually, we'd get it. I was the one that was supposed to say those things, not a kid! As it turned out, Derek's leadership was evident and lasting. He graduated from Northwestern University and then became a pilot in the Navy, serving our country. He's also got incredible kids now, and they are amazing gymnasts.

We finally got to the point of getting things turned around and wound up winning the second conference championship in the school's history. Things were looking fantastic based on the groups coming up and the elementary and middle school athletes headed our way. It was inspiring, and I knew that the next ten years at least had the potential to be banner seasons. It was a job any coach would be excited and eager to work.

So, the intelligent guy that I am, with all that basketball talent coming up, decided to look in a different direction professionally based on the urging of Mike Foster and Bob Sickles. Mike told us he was retiring, which broke the hearts of most coaches due to the tremendous job he'd done. His leaving would be a considerable loss for Gull Lake and one that could no way be filled by someone that could do the job the way Mike did. Who would be the idiot to take over that position?!

The next day, Mike called me in and told me I should apply for his job, and that those in the upper administrative end had also encouraged him to talk with me about it. Bob Sickles discussed it with me, and I thought having the opportunity of working next door to him would be great.

When Mike formally announced his retirement at our coaches meeting, it made most of us in the room kind of gulp from surprise and simply thinking that Mike would be there forever. Many of us stuck around after the meeting to gab. We talked about his retirement and all of the things he'd accomplished. It was bound to come, but we also wondered who would take over, as it was not going to be an easy thing to do.

Throughout the discussion, I remember three people who made comments to me, such as, "Are you going to apply?" and "Marc, you need to apply!" It felt good, but they may have also been saying those things because they were on drugs. I think people knew I'd helped Mike quite a bit with running events and filling in for the principal and assistant principal when they weren't in school for one reason or another, and they figured I'd be a good fit for the position.

After teaching and coaching for seven years in Gull Lake, I interviewed for the Athletic Director position and took the job. A new season was upon our family.

The first action I took was firing myself from being the head basketball coach and hiring Gary Sprague to take over the program. Gary had tremendous success in that position, and even with his unbelievable win/loss record, some people still thought he was a lousy coach. Goodness.

Gary held that position for over twenty years before being terminated by some thin-skinned people who listened to angry parents rather than standing up for a guy who had over forty years of coaching at Gull Lake in one capacity or another. He was shocked and entirely caught off guard when he went into the office for his end-of-the-year review and they told him that he'd seen his last year of coaching. Gary planned on retiring the following year and asked if he could stay one more year. Instead of letting him finish with an excellent ending to a fantastic career, they took the heartless way out and said, "No, you're fired now."

Barb Skinner was my secretary, as she had been for Mike Foster. She was excellent and did an amazing job, not just in what she did at her desk but as well as supporting me. All of our coaches liked her, and when Barb told me a few years later that she was going to retire, I felt awful. I didn't know if a replacement was possible, and as it turned out, it wasn't.

Our coaches were just as heartbroken to learn that Barb was leaving. Barb wasn't responsible for doing many of the things she did for the coaches, but she did them anyway and never said boo. She was aware of how much our coaches had to do and gladly stepped up to help, going above and beyond without question.

People don't realize all the complicated things that coaches have on their plates other than just showing up for practice and games. It's not like a college coach. Our folks work all day at another job and then have to prepare everything before and after that, so the expectations people have of high school coaches are sometimes not looked at rationally.

Even with that, the number one problem coaches have is that playing time is always the root of parents' issues. Coaches' efforts are so unknown to parents, upper administration, and other teachers. They don't understand and know everything that a coach does unless they've walked in their shoes.

With that being said, without the help and input from parents, school programs and sports would simply not exist. I was appreciative when parents wanted to involve themselves in the right way. Being a scorer at a game, usually a parent; being a ticket taker, usually a parent; being the announcer at games, usually a parent. The point is that parents provide a ton of help in so many different areas—more than the ones I've mentioned.

As stated, playing time is the major issue, as parents love their children and want to see them excel. I wanted that same thing for mine. Don't think for a minute that I haven't second-guessed a coach, and I've even told coaches that. Still, in almost every case, I supported them. Some things are out of an A.D.'s control, and their hands are tied.

That playing time issue? Encourage your child to go to the coach. What a great teaching lesson that is for your child, even if the conversation is not an easy one. If parents of kids in sports are reading this, let me give you some advice that will hopefully help each one of you. Take it if you want or throw it out with the trash.

First, always try to wait *at least* twenty-four hours to talk with the coach *if* a problem can wait. Like the good old playing time topic. It gives you time to reflect and think about the issue, and it also allows negative emotions to dissipate. Also, when you do make contact, please state from the beginning that your intent is not to have conflict but to simply try to understand and provide calm input. Reinforce that the coach is the boss, and you support that. That will go a long way in how much that coach listens to you.

These conversations can be uncomfortable at times, but if, and when, they do come up, try to take the high road. Much more will be accomplished

Second, if parents want to provide input about curriculum or other things going on in the classroom, school personnel have a responsibility to hear them out. You may not be satisfied 100%, but at least you'll be heard. As much as possible, teachers and coaches must have positive communication with parents. Again, much more can be accomplished.

MOST IMPORTANT DECISION OF MY LIFE

During my time at Gull Lake, one of my dearest friends was Mike Foster, the athletic director who preceded me in that position. He still is a treasured friend. Mike was respected as an A.D. and he was even the National Athletic Director of the Year. He did a fantastic job of building the athletic program at Gull Lake, but he got some tough news that his wife Sue contracted cancer during my first couple of years there.

Sue was also an outstanding person, who was active in the community and supportive of Mike at school. Her cancer required a bone marrow transplant that was considered experimental at the time and was going to cost around $150,000, none of which would be covered by their insurance. That's an amount a person in education doesn't have lying around.

On a Sunday afternoon, my wife and I invited five or six people to our house and discussed what the heck we were going to do to try and help Mike and Sue with the costs hanging over their heads. We decided to conduct some kind of fundraiser, but washing cars wasn't going to raise that kind of money. In the end, we figured we might as well ask people for money. We ran her story on the front page of newspapers, on the television news, and the obvious word of mouth around our community, trying to make people aware of what we were attempting to do.

We opened an account at the local bank, and people stopped there and made deposits, sent them to school in care of me, or dropped them off at our house. The response was overwhelming, and since it was during basketball season, it made it even tougher to keep up with everything. I was running on three to four hours of sleep a night, trying to teach, prepare for class, coach, be a father and husband, and spending an incredible amount of time on the venture of helping a good friend.

Peg and I were swamped with work and trying to keep track of who and how much people were giving, but we managed to keep impeccable records. Remember, the days of digital or electronic banking weren't yet upon us, so people had to write their checks out and send them in or drop them off. My new computer expertise (not quite, but it sounds good) helped us with records-keeping while always making sure there was accountability with funds.

From the day we started the effort, it took eight days to collect the money needed for the Fosters to begin the experimental bone marrow transplant. Responses came from our community as well as all over the place, and it was an event that I will certainly never forget. It also made me consider why people were contributing to the experimental bone marrow transplant, and why Peg and I were the ones that ran with it. It was the first step in things to come that would completely change my life.

Mike and Sue made the trek to a hospital in Chicago where the procedure would be done, but after a short period during the process, Sue passed away, making it a rotten end to what had become an inspiring time in the lives of so many people, including me and my wife. I didn't understand how something so horrible could happen. Why were we allowed to get our hopes up just to have the ending turn out the way it did?

Later that spring, a few of us from school decided to plan a trip to Panama City Beach, Florida for Spring Break, and we made sure it included our families. It was my second visit to Florida, the first being the Senior Class Trip with the kids from Mattawan High

School, so I wanted the second trip to be fun without having to keep track of a bunch of other people's kids—just kidding. That was an enjoyable trip, and the kids were fantastic.

My wife was given a cassette tape with the story of Pete Maravich, in his own words, that we listened to on our drive down to Panama City. Pete was one of the best basketball players ever to play the game. He was also one of my idols.

When I was a senior in college, my friend Mike Reardon and I took a trip to New Orleans to spend the week with one of our former teammates, Paul Griffin, who was playing in the NBA with New Orleans, which is now the Utah Jazz. It just so happened that Pete Maravich was also on that team, and we not only got to go into the locker room after the game and meet him, but while we were in downtown New Orleans getting a bite to eat with Grif and his wife Kim after the game, Pete was also there. I had some background with Pete, although very little, but meeting a legend and talking with him was still something special.

Roughly six months before our trip, my wife went through what I thought was a looney-tune conversion of getting to know this "Jesus Christ" guy. Little did I know that she and some great friends of ours, Mike and Pam Miller, had plotted to lay some groundwork in my life. I believe the Pete Maravich tape was part of it.

As we traveled and let the tape play, Pete talked about basketball, but he also spoke about becoming a "Born Again Christian." As I listened to Pete Maravich's emotional words, something came over me. I had to pull into a gas station to take a break; I was crying and my emotions were altogether overwhelming. I eventually shook it off, and we continued heading south.

We spent an enjoyable week in Florida with friends, and I even went parasailing, which I will never do again. I'm scared of heights, and the experience made me change my underwear when that ride was done. Once the week was over, it was time to make the trip back to Michigan and the cold weather awaiting our arrival. When we got home, we did the typical unpacking of the car and tried to get our two children, Marc and Kelli, to behave and maybe even help.

We had an answering machine on our phone, and that was a

luxury item back then. We listened to our messages, and one of them was from my wife's doctor. She'd had a pap smear just before we left for Florida. The news went something like, "Mrs. Throop, this is Doctor So-and-so's office. We wanted to let you know that your test came back positive, and the doctor would like to see you as soon as possible."

I didn't know what any of that meant, so Peg began educating me on what the results could be. Now, we'd just got through the Sue Foster thing, and thinking the worst, I folded like a little kid and began to cry and question everything I could think of. We talked about the worst-case scenario, and that wasn't fun to do.

During the conversation, Peg said to me, "Marc, if I die, I want you to get married again, but it has to be to a Christian woman."

I asked, "What's the big deal about this Christian thing? Why would I have to do that?"

She described what it meant to be a Christian, as she'd tried to a few times before. I'd always brushed her off, but she had my attention now. Peg brought out her Bible, and read the New International Version of **JOHN 3:16** to me, which states,

> *"For God so loved the world that he gave his one and only Son, that whoever believes in him shall not perish but have eternal life."*

I listened carefully, which I wasn't necessarily in the habit of always doing. I knew everlasting life sounded pretty good! Peg went on to describe what salvation was, what it meant to be "saved"—the act of believing that God sent his son to die on the cross for our sins, and then asking Him to forgive you for those sins, come into your heart, and save you from an eternity in Hell. She also told me what I needed to do to be saved and what was ahead after I was saved.

It was then I surrendered my life to Christ and became a Born Again Christian.

From that point on, things were much different for me. I was never one to back away from a good party or going to the bar with my friends to have a few beers, but I no longer had the passion to do those things. Some people think that the person who is "religious" can't have any fun and is dull. Well, I may be boring at times, but I continued having fun, just in a different way. God was changing me daily.

I still had so much to learn, and I still do to this day. But the feeling and change that I felt was terrific. It didn't mean that my life turned into some cakewalk where nothing wrong ever happened, as you'll see later, but it gave me a person in Jesus Christ that walked (and *walks!*) with me no matter what. He has forgiven my past sins, and I consciously chose to try to live my life according to what Jesus would like.

Again, it doesn't mean that I never screw up and sin. It just means that Jesus doesn't leave or forsake me, no matter what happens. And believe me, along with all other Christians, I sinned... and will sin again.

Like Peg explained when I got saved, salvation doesn't make us perfect. Some people might think Christians view themselves as better than everyone, but it is quite the opposite. However, it does guarantee us a spot in Heaven, and it forgives our shortcomings because we have been made of flesh.

Two of my college teammates from when I attended Western Michigan University some fifteen years prior, Jeff Tyson and Jim Kurzen, along with our assistant coach, Dick Shilts, were probably a little more than surprised to hear my good news. Jim and Dick were already Christians, but Jeff's conversion came once he was out of college. If it weren't for Jim Kurzen, Jeff Tyson, Dick Shilts, Pete Maravich, Mike Miller, and of course my wife Peg, my salvation would have never have happened. That's why I consider my salvation the most critical life decision I've ever made, and it's one that has taken my life on a completely different path.

Yep, some people I was friends with and had known for a long time thought that I might have gone off the deep end during my change. Some stopped wanting to be around me, as life with the brown bottle wasn't necessary. There's nothing wrong with having a drink now and again, but my life before I got saved was more drink now and again, and again, and again, and again. Alcohol was once important to me, but not any longer.

Despite that up and down period of changing friendships, more good than bad was happening. About five of us coaches at the school decided to start a Fellowship of Christian Athletes group. We met on Wednesday mornings at 6:30, an hour before school started, and everyone was invited to be a part of it. God's message of grace, forgiveness, love, and salvation was discussed every week.

We started small with maybe six or seven kids, but we grew to have over 100 kids at some of our gatherings. The group was popular but also deemed a threat to some. After the third year of gathering at that early hour, we were told that our group would have to meet off-campus; some adults were complaining about what we were saying. Spreading a message of loving everyone and allowing kids to hear how to be good people was somehow "threatening." I didn't understand, and I was hurt, but did as we were told.

That's a point to remember—just because you become a Christian doesn't mean your life will be without pain and sorrow, and it certainly doesn't mean you'll be without sin.

SAYING GOODBYE

2001 was a challenging time in my life. My dad passed away. Although he had been sick for a couple of years, I just wasn't prepared for that type of event.

The one thing we must all remember is that none of us will win at the game of life. We're all going to die, and the only thing we can do is make sure we're ready. That readiness comes from the belief that Jesus Christ is your Savior, that He died for your sins, and that you're assured of going to Heaven to be with Him. No amount of good deeds will get you there. It's simply a fact that *only* your acceptance of Him as your Savior will get you there.

Some people may say, "Well, I believe that—"

Tell me where you learned it. Anything that tells you the path to Heaven is through other means than salvation is not from the Bible. That book is evident in what we must do. I didn't make those rules or write them, but they are true. I've sinned as much as the next guy, if not worse, but God is great and has forgiven all of those past, present, and even future sins, all because of what Jesus did willingly on the cross.

Dad was always there for his kids and his wife. He coached our little league teams and went to watch us play when we got older. I can honestly tell you that I only remember once that Dad missed a game of mine in high school, and that was because of a heart scare that put him in the hospital. It got a little more challenging for him to come to all of my college games. He had to be at work on weekdays at 6:30 in the morning and many of the games were far away and on weeknights. However, there were some weeknight games where he and Mom made a three-hour trip to watch my game. If it was a Saturday game, Mom and Dad were there, no matter where the game was. During my junior year, we played at the University of Alabama, and he and my mom made the trip down there to watch us play. It was awesome!

My dad was as respected as any man, and I can genuinely say that I've never met a person who was as good and decent as Don Throop. I think about the coaches I've had in my life and continue to call my friends today, but Dad was a person you would have been amazed by. He was also a guy that treated my mom like royalty. My siblings and I sometimes laugh about that… maybe he treated her too well, as she felt that anything she wanted, she should get.

His death was tough for all of us, but it was toughest on my mother more than anyone by far. Judy, Rick, and I had our own families, but my father's death left Mom all alone in her house. She didn't adapt to the change very well and was quite miserable after he was gone. We saw her health decline during that period, and she made hospital visits more frequently due to her body beginning to fail. We felt as though the depression she was suffering from the loss of my dad was the main reason she had her episodes.

About seven years after Dad died, Mom made another trip to the hospital, and my siblings and I saw that she could no longer be left alone in her home. The doctors treating her agreed. All the options were on the table for us, and we didn't take her situation or her happiness lightly.

Finally, we found a place for her in an assisted living facility that happened to be close to where my family and I lived in Richland. It was less than a quarter-mile from my house, and I could walk there daily to see her. It was a great place, and she was well taken care of.

We were able to take her to church, the store, and to watch our kids play sports.

However, there was still the matter of missing my dad, and being a long way from her home in Romeo made the loss more painful for her. We still had the house on Bailey Street, but we knew she couldn't live there alone. Even when she was there, she complained about having to live by herself. Despite being moved to a place with other women like her, she still found it bleak and depressing.

I get it. We all felt terrible for her. Her feelings revolved around not having Dad anymore. It didn't matter where she lived; it was never going to be the same.

Even though she was doing well at her new place, loneliness and homesickness were getting to her. It was time to try and make things better for her by moving her closer to Romeo. She was involved with a group of women there that played bridge, but she couldn't even do that any longer. However, living closer might allow some of those people the opportunity to visit her.

I continue to this day wondering whether we should have had someone move in with her at the Romeo house. Then again, we talked extensively about what should take place, which, no matter what decision was made, would be bad for Mom because she missed my dad so much that no place was going to work. We hated that entire time, but we felt worse for Mom.

Rick and Judy found an excellent independent living place about a half-hour from Romeo that also allowed her to be close enough to them so they could see her at least once a week, and thankfully, their visits turned out to be more often than that. However, it just wasn't cutting the butter for her to be there, and her health began to deteriorate again. After another trip to the hospital, doctors told us she was seriously ill and that she didn't have much longer. We found another place that was an entire assisted living facility, again only a stone's throw from Rick and Judy.

Eventually, she got to the point where hospice was called in to check her daily. She stopped eating and lost so much weight. Even though the last ten years had been hard on us kids, watching Mom deteriorate was terribly painful, especially for Rick and Judy, as they'd spent much more time with her. I made the three-hour trip to her assisted living facility a couple of times a week, usually taking a day off work, driving there, and then coming back to work the next day. I'd then go back on Saturday, spend the night at a few different locations, and go back to work on Monday. Still, it was Rick and Judy that pulled the load.

It took around two weeks after hospice was called in before Mom passed away at the age of eighty-nine. One of her kids was with her the entire time, up until she passed. Again, Rick and Judy did most of the hard work because of where we all lived. All I could do was give them a break when I could.

Even though it was a long haul for everyone, she was still our mom, and we grieved knowing we wouldn't see her again. Both Mom and Dad were gone, and it was surreal to go through things for a while. I'm sure that anyone who has lost their parents feels the same way. It's just a matter of continuing with life as God has intended. Fortunately, us three siblings still talk; maybe not as much as we should, but that's something we can work on.

NEW SCHOOL LEADERSHIP

Superintendent Tom Ryan, the superintendent who hired me as a coach and teacher, retired and once he did, it seemed like there was always controversy within the system. We might have had a few more local vocals than we needed and not enough calmness that should have been easy to achieve.

Tom was the superintendent for twenty-five years, and you don't see that kind of thing happening in today's world. Parents, school boards, and staff drive superintendents out of their districts, or superintendents find new jobs that pay more. The latter is probably the more brilliant thing to do and likely advised for most administrators. The longer you're in a district, the more enemies you make. Many people in education have the best days of their careers when they first get hired. Everything else is downhill.

Our board hired my second superintendent, and we had our struggles. Even though he hired me as the A.D., I don't think he wanted to. I'll say he rarely talked to me in a cheerful tone, but oh, well—he was the boss.

He was a confident individual and began running into some trouble with folks. Following Tom Ryan was a tricky thing to do; our new person tried to make people forget who he was and ran into further conflicts with Tom's daughter-in-law, Deb Ryan, and a few members of the school board.

Deb, who was on the school board, was also on the interview team and probably significant in allowing me to become the new A.D. Following Mike was a near-impossible task because of what he had accomplished at Gull Lake so I was a little concerned, but the basketball team we had coming back was reason for more than a bit of excitement.

I was involved in the new superintendent onslaught because the school board members who disagreed with him were terrific friends of mine. I wish I would have done some things differently, but I think everyone does. Unfortunately, part of my learning experiences had not continuously increased with a few of the decisions I made. On the flip side, it takes two to tango, and things simply weren't working well. Regardless, he was a good dad, good husband, good man.

After a few years, that superintendent left for a new job in Ohio. Our board hired Mike Manor as my third Gull Lake superintendent, and the change was a good one for our extremely splintered district.

School board meetings were moved to gymnasiums to accommodate the people who attended due to the many controversies. It was a messy time for the district and the individuals involved. People were starving for someone new, and Mike's ability to not only take a stand but bring people together was tremendous. Mike let you know how he felt if he disagreed with you, but in the long run, he was still supportive.

Mike and I got along well, but when he left after a few years, we were once again in a position to hire someone new. During the interviews for the next superintendent, one of the people interviewed was a man named John Kingsnorth, who was the superintendent in Romeo that had interviewed me a few years prior and offered me the A.D. job there.

When I interviewed for the Romeo position a second time—having interviewed a few years prior to that, but withdrew after a while—I walked to that interview from my parents' house, and they were excited to think that I might be coming back. I was offered the job again, accepted it, and went so far as to move from my office at Gull Lake to the new one in Romeo. I called a meeting with the coaches at Gull Lake and told them I was leaving, and we put an offer in on a new house and put ours in Richland up for sale.

When I got to my new office in Romeo, they told me of some responsibilities that I wasn't aware of, and I noticed other things that didn't seem right. I'd prayed that I would get the job during that entire process, never stopping to ask God for His guidance and direction as to whether I should go there if offered the position, so that was yet another lesson learned. After a couple of days, I went back to Mike Manor and informed him I would not be moving, and I refused the job in Romeo.

That was at a time of tremendous confusion. I couldn't imagine leaving Gull Lake, but Peg was ready to go. She was an Army brat and moved frequently, so packing up and going didn't bother her. My kids did *not* want to move. In addition, our church, Richland Bible Church, was like another family to us and leaving that community might have been the hardest thing to do.

John Kingsnorth, who interviewed for the Gull Lake Superintendent, was a first-class individual, and I had known him for several years. He and I coached against each other and he would have made a fine superintendent, but the interview process was a big sham. We had a board member who was trouble; at one time, he said it was his job to destroy athletics at Gull Lake. Nice! He also told other board members that I gave Mr. Kingsnorth the questions prior to his interview. That didn't happen, of course, and even though John continued with his interview, he withdrew his name immediately after. I didn't find that out until afterward and almost exploded that I'd been accused of doing something so underhanded. That board member was despicable and enjoyed dividing people, and he did a pretty good job of it.

We finally hired my fourth superintendent, and being that his wife worked in the art department at WMU, he had a strong tie to the arts. He was a nice man, and his wife was also pleasant. I don't believe he showed favoritism toward those programs for a second, but I do think he was disappointed in the position due to the board makeup, especially our one nasty guy. I'm not sure too many people could have handled the mess we were going through because of the agenda-driven personalities. The superintendent was a great guy, but, in my opinion, he struggled to make progress because of that board.

Again, that person didn't last long. He retired, and my fifth superintendent was hired. There has never been a person I've worked with that was more disliked by as many people as that man was. I hate even saying that, but it's true.

He was an extremely coarse person, and if he didn't like you, you'd better watch out. Many didn't care for him because of his harsh personality, foul language, and desire for his way or no way at all. Guess who got on his bad list? I have no idea why, but he opposed me and that's the way it was from the beginning.

There was only one administrator in the district that had any sort of positive relationship with him, and that was our assistant principal. We had gone through three principals at that point, and those who followed Bob Sickles were immediately met with a challenge because people liked Bob. Bob was not a "give me all the credit" kind of guy, but he was an outstanding principal. He related to the staff, treated them well, and supported them in tough times.

I missed him when he left, as did the majority of the staff. When Bob retired, the assistant principal applied for the position. I supported him getting the job and talked with Mike Manor about it since I was on the interview team, but unfortunately, he was not in good favor with a few board members. That was a shame.

A gentleman named Dave Barry was hired, and he was an excellent academic kind of guy and a man of great character. Again, following Bob was challenging, and Dave initially got off on the wrong foot. He wanted to change the world, but people just weren't ready, including me. He lasted a couple of years before taking a job in the Detroit area. Dave and I got along well by the time he left. I wish he would have stayed, even though we had a few disagreements at the beginning of his reign. Our assistant principal, however, was excited. He saw his chance again.

Mike Manor told me he didn't care for the assistant since he wasn't supportive of the hiring following Bob Sickles, and he made it known. I felt terrible for our assistant. When Bob's successor left, Mike brought in another person for the principal position. Once again, our assistant was passed over and devastated at not getting the job.

Our assistant and I got along well, and he spent more than a few times in my office, and I in his, listening to his frustrations and seeing him literally crying over the issue. At the outset of the new principal's time, he, the assistant, and I got along well, but it wasn't that way after a while. The new guy and I had a hefty shouting match one day, but he was the better man and came to me to discuss our working relationship. We got along well after that and even got into the same Bible study at one point. We also went to a Western Michigan University/Central Michigan University football game together. Being that he graduated from CMU, I got to trash talk on the three-hour ride home when my Broncos beat his "Buffalo Chips." As for our assistant, I don't think he could get over the hurt, and our new principal felt he wasn't supported on some issues, even going as far as saying so.

That principal left shortly after, and our difficult-to-work-with person became the new superintendent. Those two didn't get along at all, but then again, most people didn't get along with that superintendent. But, his being the new superintendent allowed him to finally put our assistant into the principal's position, and he did without interviewing anyone.

Everyone was pretty happy; folks felt the assistant had paid his dues, and I was also glad because he and I had gotten along during many of the messes along the way. At times, it was difficult for me since none of the principals I'd worked for at Gull Lake felt loyalty from our assistant, and every one of them had told me. I wound up getting along with all of the principals, so there were times it wasn't easy because our assistant did not.

The new and fourth principal was okay in the early part of his run, but the support given to some of our staff members was a little shaky. I thought that non-loyalty to those staff members might have been deserved based on performance. However, at one point, he and I had a falling out with our superintendent, who didn't care for me, and he told me that he was disappointed our teams weren't winning as much as they should. Based on our success in the win/loss category, that was indeed surprising, and when I told some of my A.D. colleagues, they all said, "He doesn't like you, does he?"

The falling out with my friend who had finally become principal came when he ripped into me during an evaluation and recommended my contract not be renewed. I knew he was under stress; he was friends with the superintendent, and I have no doubt that the superintendent told him to give me a poor review. The things said to me the day of my evaluation were unbelievable, and I was not a happy camper with his inability to speak the truth.

Most people knew the current principal and superintendent had their relationship, and many joked about it... sometimes right in front of him. The principal was a good father and a good guy. He was a "move along as normal" kind of administrator, but I thought he'd done some decent things. There were other traits that some felt were better. Again, he was a wonderful guy, but I was disappointed he hadn't told me the truth behind that evaluation.

"Mr. Wonderful" finally retired after six years in the district, and it almost felt like a cause for celebration, with many going out to rejoice like it was New Year's Eve. People were hungry for a person who would treat them well while leading our district in a direction we could rally around. Following several interviews, a man was hired to become our new superintendent, and he started with a ton of respect. He was a kind man, which was a new life for most of us.

After a couple of years of having yet another superintendent (my sixth), the principal decided to "retire" from the district... even though he did find new employment as a principal at a neighboring school. Thus, another principal (my fifth!) was hired, one that a lot of us knew. He was the principal at a school we'd rivaled in sports for decades before they fell on hard times due to circumstances that were entirely out of their hands. The big General Motors plant got shut down, meaning many families moved. Then the Kalamazoo Public Schools created The Promise, which allows kids that graduate from there to have their tuition paid at any college or university in Michigan—an incredible gift, but in the world of our rival, it didn't help. They had some excellent people there, but many left for those two reasons, and enrollment began heavily declining.

That principal was an interesting hire. He was one of the final three people to make the cut for the position, but was the third choice of the committee. The first choice didn't accept the job; the second choice was skipped over in favor of the new person because the superintendent felt from the beginning that *his* choice would be *the* choice. And so, the superintendent made the call to hire him. I had zero problems with that since he was the boss. Besides, it wasn't a case of completely "out of left field" decision-making.

NEW FAMILY MEMBERS

My son, Marc, was about to get married, and that officially made me old.

Marrying Lyndsie was great for all of us. She's a perfect mom who does so much with our granddaughters. As I said, she had a child from a previous relationship, Annie, and they now have two more, Natalie and MerryJane. Lyndsie works, takes care of three kids, and keeps all their appointments straight.

She's an incredibly hard worker. Her family ran a bar/restaurant called The Barking Frog, so they decided to get married at The Frog. Peg and I often used the excuse, "Hey, let's go see Lyndsie and her mom, Tammy, at work!" because they had great food and large portions. That's my kind of place.

Their wedding was a fun day and one that I'm certainly glad happened. Her family is incredible, and we are blessed to have them as in-laws.

ACCOMPLISHMENTS AT GULL LAKE

hile I was at Gull Lake, many positive accomplishments for the entire school district and community were made. It's not my intent to say, "Way to go, Marc!" when I discuss the things below. Still, I genuinely believe that the district saw more athletic facility improvements during my time than any other in the school's history, and they had more success with athletic teams and program improvements.

Those things included:

- New $100,000 press box built over my first year as A.D. I joke with Mike Foster sometimes about the fact that he began the process of trying to get a new press box built, got a lot of it in place, and then retired, leaving me—a rookie A.D.—to move forward with things. I was named A.D. in late spring 1995, and the old press box was torn down at that same time. Mike, Mike, Mike! He and I are still great friends to this day, so I can joke about that with him.
- New artificial turf, costing about $700,000; those funds came from both private and school funding.

- New first-class softball/baseball dugouts, which cost much more than I imagined. I got an idea of the funds we needed by talking with our coaches, but people above me wanted to make things look like our new expensive school. Thus, a project I imagined costing roughly $75,000 turned into one around $300,000. As it turned out, there wasn't enough money, so we had to sacrifice some details, like getting decent bleachers. The ones we got looked great, but they were highly inadequate and the cost was still high.
- New softball/baseball press boxes; again, of excellent quality with P.A. systems, ample storage, and other niceties. These were part of the above project and were included in that cost.
- New scoreboards at every outdoor facility, including baseball, softball, football and soccer, indoor scoreboards for basketball/volleyball/wrestling, and twenty-five-second play clocks for the football field. 100% of the funding came from the grocery chain Meijer.
- Pathway of Pride, a new $350,000 building at the football field that has a concession stand, ticket booth, storage, and a Sports Boosters store.
- The new Hall of Fame, which has been highly successful, and I started it with the intention to induct three people every three years. We installed five the first year, and I didn't want to have an induction until Mike Foster could be eligible and be a part of the first class of inductees.
- All-Sports Award, presented to one school every year based on their success in our athletic conference. If you finished first in, say, football, you're awarded twenty points, eighteen for second, and so on. At the end of the year, points for each school are totaled to determine the winner of the award. We won that award for twenty-eight straight years, and that success caused other league schools to give us the boot from that league. They said it

was because of our size, but that wasn't why. An A.D. told me a couple of years later that it was our success. That award became a tremendous sense of pride, but the other schools didn't like us winning it every year. I understood; it became an uncomfortable topic for me at our league A.D. meetings. After getting tossed out of that league, we transitioned into the league made up of the largest enrollment schools in the area, but we were the smallest school. They did not have an All-Sports Champion, but I couldn't help myself and kept track of it anyway. We would have won for the first three years, even though we were the little guys on the block. I didn't dare tell people about that.

- We were the first school in Michigan to receive the Scope Award, given to the school with the best overall outlook on what high school athletics was supposed to be like in the state.
- We were the first school in Michigan to be awarded the MIAA (Michigan Interscholastic Athletic Administrators Association) / MHSAA (Michigan High School Athletic Association) Exemplary Athletic Award, given to the school that was determined to be exemplary in many different areas. This award is the ultimate award for a school to receive.
- I was elected President of the MIAAA, which carried a five-year term of different levels of responsibilities.
- I was named Regional Athletic Director of the Year.
- I was inducted into the Wolverine Conference Distinguished Service group, which is essentially their version of a Hall Of Fame.

There are other accomplishments that improved our athletic programs, of course. These were indeed not the results of only my doing, but that of so many others who assisted me along the way. I believe they're important and I'm proud that I was a part of them, especially given some circumstances that came up later in my career that cast me in a negative light. I'll tell you about them, too, but not just yet.

As we continue along, there will, unfortunately, be some things mentioned about a few individuals who I believe will be quite offended due to their lack of judgment and fear of standing up to those with influence, authority, and power. But, based on what you're going to read, the things I've listed above should give you an idea of what general accomplishments all of us in the Gull Lake community can honestly take credit for.

On the Sunday afternoon of our state's 2010 Annual A.D. Conference, voting between the two candidates running for president—myself and Cody Inglis—was announced. Cody was a top-notch A.D. and an even better person than me. He's now one of the assistant directors of the MHSAA, which is the governing body for all schools in Michigan. When it was announced that I had won the election, I was excited even though I thought Cody would have done a great job. He came from the northern part of Michigan, which doesn't have as many schools as the southern part of the state, which may have been why I won.

That election requires runners to serve as the Recording Secretary the first year, Second Vice President the second year, First Vice President the third year, and then the President. When we went to the conference that fourth year, I received the President's ring and took the helm in the top spot as president. On the way home from that conference, I was excited to start serving and eager to tell everyone back home.

26

FIRST RETIREMENT

During the 2012-2013 school year, I grew physically and mentally tired of being an A.D. and all the things that came with the position. The long hours, ranging from sixty to eighty hours a week, were physically taxing. Hauling items around and often standing in inclement weather, amongst other mentally draining issues, took their toll on my health. Although 95% of the parents I had interaction with in education were rock-solid and supportive, I can say that when the phone in my office rang, 80% of the time it was with bad news regarding various issues, including the most dreaded parental complaints about playing time.

I remember sitting in our press box one night at a soccer game and listening to someone talk about a bullying conference they'd attended and all the things that bullying included. Now understand, bullying *does* happen, and it's an issue that should never be tolerated and should be dealt with immediately. One of the areas brought up was that of teachers bullying students, and I thought to myself, *Oh, boy, here we go.*

Examples they gave of a teacher bullying a student included things like a teacher rolling their eyes, raising their voice, or using a harsh tone. I kept my mouth shut; they were a great person and a school board member, but I couldn't buy into those things being bully tactics. I did, however, ask them about parental bullying toward teachers, coaches, and administrators, and they said, "Well, that just doesn't happen very often."

That pretty much says it all regarding people simply not understanding what happens with education and parental involvement unless you're in the trenches. I explained that parental bullying happens almost daily, especially in sports, due to it being an area where emotions run high and that communities have some people who know more about doing the coaches' jobs than the coaches do. Just ask a coach. I asked the person what they thought about that, and their response was, "That's just bad behavior."

Again, keep in mind that the person I was talking with was a good—no, *great*—person, and I absolutely believe they had the best intentions. But some people just don't get it. Listen, folks, teachers are the bosses of their classroom, and coaches are the bosses of their teams. Parents should have zero say in regards to *most* things that happen. That, I'm sure, will touch a few nerves the wrong way for some.

I believe learning what authority means is much better understood at a younger age. Why do we wonder why children don't have as much respect for teachers and coaches anymore when parents are on the phone telling their educators how badly they're doing their jobs, and then sitting at the dinner table reiterating to their child how bad of a job their coaches and teachers are doing? I don't care if you think the coach made a mistake. Just don't let your kids hear you talking about it negatively. Let kids bear the brunt of a scolding every once in a while and allow them to grow up.

After wondering how to slow down for quite some time in my job, I drafted a proposal for our superintendent. It would allow me to retire, work during the day, and then have an event manager handle the night activities with the exception of the Friday night football games, which I would continue. I'd collect my retirement from the public school's retirement fund, which teachers are mandated to put some of their wages into for their entire career. I would also collect what the school was permitted to pay me so that

I'd bring home the same amount of money while being a little kinder to my body. In addition, the school district would save a lot of money, so I believed it was a win for everyone involved.

Discussions concerning the buyout got more defined as time went by, and I was hopeful of things working out. I knew the superintendent thought it was a good idea as well. He told me it made a lot of sense and that others should consider it, and he'd talk to members of the school board about it.

In the spring of 2013, I was named President of the MIAAA at our annual conference. Excitement on my end was no doubt present, and it was great that my son Marc, along with my other son Noah, and my wife, were on hand to see me placed in that position. Josh was at school in Alabama and Kelli worked in Chicago, so they couldn't make it. I was looking forward to going back to school and sharing that excitement.

I got a call on the way home and was asked to stop by our central office. I went into the business manager's office and we talked a little before the conversation turned to the buyout. We then went to the superintendent's office and in that meeting, he said that the board had approved my proposal, which was great news. The bad news was that he also told me that if I didn't take it, the next year would be my last—I would not have a contract extension.

Seeing that I was close to the end of my career in education, I was mortified, confused, and dumbfounded by what he was saying, and I wanted to know why. Turns out there were a couple of reasons.

He stated that our Sports Boosters President had gone to him and said that the school needed to change my position because I didn't want our boosters paying an assistant coach a stipend. According to MHSAA rules, it would have been illegal to do so. This guy was used to getting his way, but when it didn't happen, he wanted me fired. I had gotten along with him despite numerous people telling me not to trust him, as he would "stab you in the back." Shame on me.

Another reason involved an incident that had happened a few years prior to my proposal. We had a varsity wrestling coaching position available. There was a J.V. coach that I liked and who had done an excellent job for us at that level as well as another applicant, who used to be the coach. He and I had not done well together in the past. He was insubordinate to my directions and someone that many other coaches on our staff didn't care for or trust due to his coarse nature and personality. I wasn't high on him taking over and wanted the J.V. coach hired.

Our J.V. coach emailed me and the wrestling parents, and I responded, asking for the names of a couple of parents that would be good to sit in on interviews, as I wanted them to go well. A couple of days later, our volleyball coach—who was married to the previous coach I didn't want hired—came into my office, shut the door, and proceeded to scream at me. She told me she had no respect for me. Oh, boy.

We had gotten along fairly well up until that point. In fact, I'd hired her several years before that incident. I'd always hoped she would be the next Gull Lake A.D. after me, and I had told many people the same thing. However, that incident put tension in our relationship.

I went to our principal and told him what happened. My actions were determined to be wrong, but to this day, I'd still want the person I thought was right for us hired. So be it.

Our principal called our superintendent so that we could explain the situation. Don't forget, this was the same superintendent that hired the principal—the third choice of the three finalists, who just so happened to get the job because the first man turned down the principal position and the second was skipped over so the superintendent could hire who he wanted. When we spoke to our superintendent, he reprimanded me, saying it was an inappropriate thing to do, but he gave me his word that he would end it.

Sounded good. I took the correction to heart. The situation was over, right?

Later in the spring, he called me into the office and told me that he had to wait until school got out to renew my contract because someone was bugging him about the wrestling coach issue. I wasn't pleased, but he gave me his word once again and told me no more would come of the situation. He then said, "I hate that guy," referring to the coach that didn't get the job, and you could tell he had an "active board member" giving him some problems.

But it wasn't the end. As I said, when I returned from the conference, he told me that the next year would be my last. He brought up the wrestling issue *again*, claiming it was also a factor. That made it the third time he had brought it up and broke his word. At that point, my respect for him made me reconsider things. I knew it was simply a matter of him not telling certain people to back off.

So there we were; more examples of people butting into situations combined with a superintendent who didn't like standing up to others with influence. My secretary told me that before that superintendent was hired, she'd called his previous school and the criticism of him there was that he refused to stand up to those with money and power. Sounds like they had him pegged.

In the end, I took the buyout. He told me he'd put in a request with the board that I be able to work two more years so I could fulfill my responsibilities with the MIAAA. I thanked him for that. I knew he was looking for that "thank you" from me because he believed he had supported me—and I supposed he'd given me some support. Thus, two more years, and I would be done at Gull Lake.

Before going further, let me tell you that this guy was a decent person and well-liked. His personality truly was conducive to kindness.

27

KIDS AND MISTAKES

One of the more difficult times in a parent's life is when something terrible happens to one of their children, whether or not it's their fault. The reality is that at some point, our kids will do something that proves to us that their decision-making process isn't always the best or how we want it to go, kind of like when we were all kids. It's gut-wrenching and causes stress, but if you have kids, it's going to happen.

Heck, I did that with my parents. I look back at the things I did and shiver sometimes, but I didn't get caught with some of the dumb choices I made. Still, the parent in each of us expect our kids to be perfect, but it just doesn't happen.

The conversations we had with our children were usually pretty low-key in terms of our tone, but they knew they were in trouble and sensed when the hammer was about to come down. It's not that we, as parents, were angry or mad (well, maybe a little), but more of a feeling that our little boy or girl was getting older. After a bit of conversation, we tried to educate them. The consequence of being at home was one they accepted without hesitation.

Little kids, little problems. Big kids...

Not only was I a parent, but I was also the athletic director. That put me in a tough spot. When sports kids got in trouble, there were consequences from an athletic standpoint, even if what they did to get in trouble didn't happen at school or during the sports season. It was my job to gather facts about the entire situation, which took some time. If other kids were involved, I called their parents and hoped they'd be appreciative. Fat chance sometimes!

An incident I went through early in my A.D. years reminded me of what I think was one of the worst decisions I made at Gull Lake as an athletic director.

Earlier, I mentioned some parents that were wonderful regarding their perspective on high school sports and their roles. Two of those parents, who I won't name, walked into my office one day with their son and informed me that they had come home to find their kid and another boy sitting around the dinner table, and each of them had a couple of beers. The rule at that point was to suspend someone for twenty percent of the season for their first offense, and I stuck to the rule.

Now, there was a family—an outstanding family at that—reporting their son's mistake because they knew it broke the rules. He was an honor student, captain, and one of the finest kids at Gull Lake, and I gave him the harshest punishment possible over two beers!

Yes, there are consequences for actions, but the penalty did not fit the crime on that one, and it was a big mistake on my part. I flat-out screwed that one up. His punishment should have been far lesser than what I dished out. Even though it was the rule, common sense was not used. We eventually changed that, but what a regret.

Another case involved one of my children. I knew people would scrutinize how I handled the situation, so after getting all the information, I went to our principal and told him I was self-reporting my child and the others involved, who were on another school's team. He agreed that he and our superintendent should handle it instead of me.

Typically, a parent could say that they were not going to rat on other kids, but in my position as the A.D., I knew there were kids who had broken rules, and I had to deal with that from a school standpoint. Looking back, it's kind of funny because when I told our principal that he, along with our superintendent, were probably the people who needed to decide what to do, he said, "Marc, can you tell me what I'm supposed to do?"

I let him know what the first offense consequences were, but if a parent were to self-report their child, we reduced their suspension to ten percent. I'd learned from my previous experience as well as other occasions when kids made unwise decisions, and we'd already changed the method of consequence. I thought to myself that everything was taken care of, but I found out otherwise.

The superintendent called me and our principal and informed us that some parents had called him, one of which was a school board member, and let him know how outraged they were that the kids had different punishments, and that the consequences might ruin their kids' future. They wanted me fired and my child off the team for good.

Believe it or not, the superintendent initially agreed my child should be removed from the team but not the other kids involved, as they would be able to serve their standard suspension. That tells you a little something about things nowadays in regards to parental support of school staff decision-making. Giving kids consequences for their mistakes was a terrible part of my job, but more significant problems would have arisen had I not. The crazy thing is that the kids of the disgruntled parents were terrific and remain friends with my child to this day.

After our principal and I talked some reason into him, the superintendent finally decided my child would receive the same discipline. If I had not reported the situation with all of the information, I might understand the need for me to be reprimanded or even terminated. Needless to say, I was once again amazed that he was so ready to cave into the vocal people of "influence" instead of rationally looking at the situation, standing up to them, and doing the right thing. I know he had his bosses, but it was frustrating to know backdoor conversations influenced his decisions.

I understand the politics and dynamics of the school board hierarchy. Still, I don't agree with it, and I was never very good about the political aspect when someone wanted me to do something that wasn't the right thing. That got me in trouble at times, especially at the end of my career, but nevertheless, I consider him a good man. I liked working for him most of the time.

Having been in the education and coaching field, I often faced the difficult task of disciplining kids for wrong choices like drinking, smoking, and a wide range of other offenses. If someone broke a rule or if the law was broken, most of the time, I had to take action when I didn't want to. I wasn't afraid to do so, but there were several times I thought the punishment handed out according to our handbook wasn't necessarily the right course of action.

Drinking alcohol and smoking marijuana seemed to be the most popular offenses, both of which I don't condone for underage kids. If someone got caught doing something like that when I was young, the coach ran the living heck out of you, and that, more than anything, was a deterrent. You could continue to be involved in an activity, which was a positive. A handbook wasn't needed because the coach could decide how to handle you.

My thoughts? It was probably when whiney parents got involved and thought physical discipline like that was abusive that caused more rules than were needed in some school handbooks.

Even worse was when a parent disciplined their child at home and we'd have to get involved. If a parent was taking action, then why should we? Let's keep the job of raising kids in the hands of parents when we can. Remember, just because your child makes a mistake doesn't mean they're bad. If others judge you or your child because of it, they're the ones with the problem.

One example came when I had to call a girl to my office after she was found drinking. Following that conversation, I got a call from her father, and he was upset (an understatement), having already dealt with it at home. He wanted us to stay out of it. I understood, but it was the rule I had to follow.

I would have loved to have said, "Thanks for doing that, and I appreciate you handling it." Even though that parent was *not* happy with me, he was one of the people to reaffirm his support for me when all heck broke loose in 2015, but we'll get to that later.

28

PEG'S HEALTH

The fall of 2014 found me looking forward to retiring from education the following spring. I intended to find another job, one that wasn't as taxing as being an athletic director. It would also mark the end of a thirty-eight-year career in education.

Getting involved in leadership organizations was a direction I thought about, but I knew it had to be some place that would yield a positive result for others, especially kids. Peg and I would have a lot more free time together, even though we still had Noah at home, who wasn't graduating until the spring of 2017.

During that time, Peg started to feel a little goofy. She had symptoms that included less strength in her right hand, not being able to swing her right arm when she walked, stumbling with her right foot more frequently, and a complete loss of her sense of smell. Her living at home with Noah and me, well… sometimes that no-smell thing was a blessing for her. Smoking cigars and farting were going to work! However, it had to be looked into, so she went and had several tests run.

There was fear that possible multiple sclerosis or ALS would be an outcome. When the dust cleared and all the tests were taken, she was diagnosed with Parkinson's disease. It impacted her, but I tried my best to stay upbeat and not show how much it bothered me. Peg is a rock, and when someone asks her how she's doing, she is exceptionally positive. No pun intended, but she is a real trooper.

She began taking the medications that would help limit the effects, but something else was also bugging her that wasn't in the category of Parkinson's. Severe back problems forced her to slow down, and the pain, at times, was unbearable. Her doctor referred us to a specialist who might be able to do physical therapy along with some pain relief tactics, which she did, but nothing seemed to work.

After a period of treatment, the doctor did an MRI and found she had a pinched nerve in her lower back. To this day, I can't spew the medical terminology they used, but I know she was in a tremendous amount of pain. Surgery was an option, but her dad and my dad had back surgery, neither of which turned out well.

At that point, she began injections to relieve the pain, but she could only get them three times a year. The injections initially helped, but within a month, the pain was back. After about a year, the shots had no effect whatsoever. Some of her friends and I suggested that she strongly consider surgery.

Spinal stenosis in the back was the official diagnosis. Peg decided to hold off on surgery since it was coming close to the busiest time of the year at work for her, and when she was at work, she did a lot of manual labor and standing on her feet.

Where did she work? Well, that's a blessing God gave to her and so many others, and the story is pretty remarkable. Let's backtrack a bit and I'll tell you about it.

29

TASTE OF HEAVEN

T he story of Taste of Heaven is unique, and one that certainly shows what living in the greatest country can provide for someone who wants to do something. Having the freedoms and opportunities that we do should never be taken for granted. For those that scream when something doesn't go their way? Try some other place and see how blessed we are.

One Sunday in early 1999, we went to church at Richland Bible Church, just like any other Sunday. At the time, it was a rapidly growing congregation with around 2,000 people attending weekly. We loved our church and the fact that it was a Bible-teaching church. The people and pastor who were there made it even better.

We sat listening to the sermon that day. The lesson was that of the three talents, and our pastor described the three different scenarios it dealt with. The *Reader's Digest* version of the story is that the master gave three servants some money. One doubled it, one increased it by ten times, and one hid it. The servant who hid the money had it taken from him. Moral: If you don't use your talent, you lose your talent.

What happened next is something most people might never imagine happening in a church. Envelopes were handed out to anyone in the congregation who wanted one that promised to come back in November with their story of what they did with what was in their envelope and how it was invested. Peg and I both took one.

Those envelopes contained either a one, five, ten, twenty, or fifty dollar bill, and over $7,000 was handed out that day. I know—crazy, right? Typically, churches ask for money.

Rules were not shared on what to do with it, only the encouragement to take action. The pastor suggested that those taking an envelope could invest in several ways. Maybe buy someone lunch and share the Gospel or provide a homeless person a meal. When we got home, my wife opened her envelope and found a ten-dollar bill. Like a good wife and mother, she put the money on the refrigerator door only to have it sit there until May. Handed out in January, it took a while for her to come up with something.

One day, she determined she better do something with it, so she went out and bought some caramel and chocolate and made four different containers of chocolate-drizzled caramel corn. She then brought those to school and *told* each of the four secretaries that they needed to give her five dollars each for a bag of the stuff. How cool is it that she took her ten dollars and turned it into twenty, making a nice story?!

Well, a couple of the people who bought it asked her if she'd make some more. They then shared it with others, and I'm sure you can guess the rest of the story.

In November, when stories were told about what other members of the congregation had done with their money, Peg turned in over $800 from the money she received in January. End of the story, right? Not quite. People wanted more, which I have to admit, Peg's concoction was darn good.

She asked the church if she could use their kitchen and started a nonprofit business called Taste of Heaven. We'd just had Noah, so she would throw him in one of those backpack carriers, and, with him in tow, make her caramel corn. Pretty soon, the church kitchen got too small. One man who went to our church mentioned that the Kalamazoo Gospel Mission had a building that wasn't being used and she should look into it.

The business activity was fair to begin with, but when the Christmas season came along… oh, my goodness. Customers were flocking in, buying like crazy, forcing our entire family and some other extremely loyal volunteers to help out to try and keep up with demand. Per Peg's request, some of the homeless people at the mission were given an opportunity to help and learn work skills. I still remember the first two Christmases when we were making caramel corn on Christmas Eve and still not able to keep up with the demand.

It was never her or our intent to keep the money. It was truly God at work, allowing us to help His Kingdom. Therefore, all of the profits went right to the Gospel Mission, along with our church. Peg made a wage, although it was minimum wage.

The business continued growing, but after a few years, the Mission determined that running a business was not their purpose, so they decided they would no longer be a part of it. It was an amicable split, and the executive director of the Kalamazoo Gospel Mission, who is an outstanding man as well, wished us the best. That left Peg looking for a new place to turn over profits to, and lo and behold, another person in our church, Mark Jevert—who was the Kalamazoo Area Youth For Christ Executive Director—approached her.

He knew the entire venture was a God-thing and thought the opportunity to partner with Taste of Heaven could benefit many. He was essentially looking for his "Girl Scout Cookie" for Youth For Christ, and he had heard that the Mission was going to split from Peg. Peg took the business and *gave* it to YFC to keep all the profits. That's right—simply handed it over without getting a dime. She allowed them to do with it what they chose. Peg continued to manage the place, but it was a clean and legal way for YFC to be the beneficiary of Taste of Heaven.

The Mission building they were still using and paying rent to eventually became too small, and the need for a better facility and location was a must. A building became available at an excellent site where lots of traffic and more business showed potential. It was expensive, but much better suited to their needs.

Youth For Christ's mission is to reach kids for Christ, and to love them whether in the juvenile home or on the streets. They find them mentors and share the love of Christ by meeting them where they are in life. Peg admitted that marketing was not her strong suit and that she needed help, so YFC hired a full-time manager named Lynn Russher. Lynn was fantastic, and she and Peg became great friends.

The business is still going strong today. They have now moved into an even bigger building and have a website. Taste of Heaven at drizzled.org. Check it out.

The success is God's. He put Peg in a situation that she didn't want and wasn't looking for, but she followed His lead. You're probably saying to yourself, "Just how much are they making?" From that ten dollars until now, Taste of Heaven has returned profits of between $500,000 and $1,000,000 to be used in the mission field, helping kids at risk. I think that's a pretty neat thing, and so do most who know the story.

Many have said that Peg was crazy—she could have had all that money! Well, we did do a lot of things with the money, as it's been a way to help our church, the Gospel Mission, and YFC to be able to help the youth in our area. As she says, "It's always been God's business."

Like everything else we have in our marriage, we walked hand in hand in making the decisions on how to deal with that season of our lives and what happened with Taste of Heaven.

The bad news is that Peg's work was labor intensive, and her health wasn't allowing her to continue doing something so strenuous. She would come home after work and have to hold onto the house to get in. We planned for her to stop working at the end of the Christmas season 2016.

I was concerned, as were our kids, about how she was going to handle work during the regular Christmas season, being that she worked about sixty hours a week. She backed off a little in the off-season, only working twenty to thirty hours a week, but since Peg was in so much pain, I couldn't imagine how she would make it to the end.

Youth For Christ hired a great guy named Scott Pease, and he has done a fantastic job. Peg and Scott worked well together for the short period she was there after he came on board. In December, Peg finally had back surgery and felt so good after it that she stayed on and worked another year.

30

FEBRUARY 25, 2015

The next phase of this book is difficult to write for many reasons, and one of them is because the people involved are such great people. Remember, Peg had been diagnosed with Parkinson's the previous fall, and now I would experience something I never imagined could happen. We've all had tough days in our lives, but I couldn't have guessed for a minute what was coming or that it would change the course of our entire family's lives.

Peg's medical issues meant we had to get used to knowing that things were changing for us. I would be retiring altogether from being an A.D. in a few months, which turned out to be a good thing. I had an abbreviated work schedule so that I could help more around the house and also be able to spend much more time with my wife and family.

As the Gull Lake Athletic Director, I was so entrenched in all that occurred with the school that, for me, it became just like another child. When something terrible happened, I felt sick to my stomach. I'm sure most A.D.s have had that same feeling. It's the nature of working a tremendous number of hours, the passion ingrained in your head, and that you can't get it out of your mind.

When you're an athletic director, there will be decisions made that don't sit well with people, and you'll make enemies due to those decisions without trying. The last thing I wanted to do was to make enemies, but it wasn't my choice to make it that way.

My complete retirement from Gull Lake was only about four months away and drawing closer every day. I wasn't going to coast out, but I did turn more responsibilities over to our event manager. I knew they would be a good fit for the job and would probably be the new Athletic Director once I was gone. I wasn't the one hiring the next A.D., but giving more responsibilities to the event manager would help a great deal in them getting the position. It also allowed me to transition into retirement more smoothly while still keeping things going in a direction that enabled coaches, parents, and students to feel like we weren't missing a beat.

The person was hired and became our event manager when I "retired" the first time and got the buyout. Three people were interviewed and several of our coaches hoped that a guy named Ben Armer would get the job, as Ben was an outstanding man of character, and I knew that his presence would be suitable for the position. However, he did not get the job. Thankfully, an extremely capable individual was hired. Coaches knew who it was and were also pleased.

I felt things were going well, right up until February 25, 2015. That date turned out to be the worst day of my life.

Our principal called me late that morning and said the superintendent wanted to see us in his office. I asked him what was going on, and he said he didn't want to tell me, so I planned for bad news. Maybe a coach had hit a kid or was having an inappropriate relationship with a student, or perhaps even something tragic had happened. My main concerns were that my family was okay, and I also wondered if someone had accused me of something. Still, I thought the relationship between me and the principal was good enough that he would tell me if it was something too crazy.

I arrived at the central office and found the principal, superintendent, and our assistant superintendent of finance in the superintendent's office. After some small talk, I was told that the conversation we were about to have would be difficult. Since I didn't know what was going on, I was a little anxious. A lump formed in my throat and a pit sat in my stomach.

The superintendent then asked me, "How long have you been taking money from the district?"

I sat there with a blank look on my face, unable to say anything and more than a little confused. Being that I'd never taken anything I wasn't supposed to, I genuinely wasn't sure what was up. He forcefully told me that he knew I was taking money from the ticket box and again asked how long I had been doing it.

I told him, "I don't know what you're talking about."

I knew at that point something significant was going on, and my heart started pounding. It didn't take long for me to get to the point of shock and disbelief.

In a loud and upset tone, he once again stated he *knew* I was doing it, and it "pissed him off." I'd never seen him so mad. He explained that the money in the cash box had been counted the night before at the girls' basketball game and again that morning. The money I'd turned in was different from what had been counted.

Wait, *that's* what made everyone so upset? I was relieved, knowing the situation could be easily explained. I told them all that yes, of course I had taken some cash from the previous night's game sales, but only to pay for the pre-season coaches meeting that was going to be held that very night.

At the beginning of every sports season, we held a meeting to remind coaches about what I thought were important points and introduce new coaches. I got our pizzas from Kolligs Korner Market. It was owned by a former Sports Boosters President, and I bought from there to support him and his business. However, the owner told me a couple of years prior that he wanted me to pay him in cash; it simply took too long for him to get a check from the school.

The school's payment policy could sometimes take a few weeks to complete. Also, checks were not printed on approval; those that came out for that purpose were only printed every two weeks. If the central office approved a payment at the beginning of a check-writing period, it could possibly take almost a month for a check to get to its destination from the time it was sent out. Some cases were determined to be emergencies, and checks could be cut relatively quickly within a few days, but I didn't think pizzas and supplies, cookies, chips, and pop qualified as an emergency. Without question, that system was broken, and I certainly understood why a vendor wanted to be paid with cash from the school as opposed to waiting so long for payment.

Regardless, the superintendent said that he didn't believe me. He had "proof" I'd stolen before—a very questionable piece of documentation.

During the meeting, the three of them looked at a document of some kind, but when I asked to see it, I was denied that request. I never saw what they called evidence, but found out later that the document was a spreadsheet my secretary and our event manager had compiled. They took the spreadsheet to the principal and claimed there was a problem. Instead of asking me what may be wrong—which would have been the professional and Biblical thing to do being that we attended the same church—they went right past me.

My secretary said she was concerned after I turned in my game report from our wrestling regionals the previous Thursday, which was different from the report our event manager turned in the next day. It was easy to see why it was different—she had listed the starting cash at $200 while I had indeed put in $300. Uh-oh. How'd that happen?

Usually, I entered $200 for starting cash unless I thought the crowd would be more significant, which a wrestling regional would be. I thought nothing about it at the time, but that's where I made a mistake. I didn't adjust the starting cash on the report from $200—which was the default value on all my reports—to $300. Therefore, my secretary went to the event manager and not me.

A few of the people who supported me told me they'd heard her talk ill of me, but this one was over the top. Again, nobody ever showed me that spreadsheet during the meeting, which was supposed to be considered evidence of my so-called wrongdoing.

The rest of that meeting was confusing and uncomfortable. I wasn't sure why I was still being accused of stealing when I had been a loyal employee for twenty-seven years. I'd explained what had happened in detail, and despite their "evidence," my statement was honest.

Early on during that February 25th forty-five-minute meeting nightmare meeting, I was informed I would be terminated. The superintendent also said that he had contacted the school lawyer and law enforcement. I figured it was best to keep my mouth shut as much as possible other than trying to explain myself, especially when I'd already been told no one believed me.

Now, I know our superintendent was good at his job, but from the time he was made aware of what happened that morning around 9:30, he'd called the lawyer, called the police, told them all what was going on, and conducted a "thorough investigation..." all by 11:00. That didn't seem to make much sense to me.

I left that meeting and headed to my car. The principal followed me out and got all of my keys. I was visibly shaken, a basket case because of what had happened, but through my tears, I reiterated that I hadn't done what I was being accused of.

As I left our central office that day and drove home, I could not have felt any worse. I cried and worried about the effects my termination would have on my family. I immediately called Peg and told her that she needed to come home from work right away, but I didn't tell her what it was concerning. That night, we called a family meeting with my wife, two of my sons, and my daughter. Josh was still in school at the University of Alabama, so he couldn't be there and had no idea anything was going on until after our meeting when Kelli called him.

I was more than just a mess, and I couldn't believe what was happening. My emotions were beyond rattled. It was a nightmare I was hoping to wake up from. I couldn't even talk on the phone with anyone. In fact, for the next couple of weeks, if my phone rang, I wouldn't answer it unless the call was from maybe two or three people. I texted my brother and sister and told them to Google my name and explained a few things to them without going into specifics. However, I still couldn't talk with them directly at length.

It was then I knew I had to stop questioning everything and go to God and turn it over for Him to handle as **EPHESIANS, CHAPTER 3**, had taught me. I didn't stop being depressed and disheartened, but I continued to ask God to take control, begging for healing through my prayers, and asking Him to comfort me.

On the night of our family meeting, my daughter Kelli, who is a go-getter, handled a lot in regards to talking with people. She is much like me in that when a crisis arises, she's good about taking charge and finding solutions. Kelli called a friend of hers who used to practice law but had since started his own business, and she asked who we should contact.

He referred us to a gentleman named Chris Tracy, who I knew and thought highly of, and called him a friend. Since Chris was on the board of the school's foundation, he couldn't help us, but he did refer us to another attorney, Jim Shinar. Jim took my daughter's call and set us an appointment with him the very next day.

The following day was no better in terms of how I felt. Peg didn't go into work the rest of the week. She was aware I could not be left alone. It isn't comfortable to even admit, but I own a registered handgun for home protection, and my son, Marc, took it home with him after our meeting the night before, just in case my emotions worsened. Marc is a tough kid who wasn't overly worried about what the outcome of my scenario would be and eventually laughed to think the whole issue happened.

I didn't want to leave the house, but Peg had an errand she had to take care of, so I drove her. On the way, we called my doctor's office and talked to a nurse to ask if he could prescribe something powerful to help me with my emotions. The nurse asked me to come in and speak with the doctor, but I wasn't talking to anyone at that point. My wife was my voice, and she told the nurse to have the doctor read the paper and he'd understand. Ten minutes later, the nurse called back, and my prescription for Xanax was ready for us to pick up.

I took those things like they were candy, as well as other

medication for anxiety. Dangerous? You bet. Needed? You bet. Thankfully, I didn't become hooked and fall into a place that so many others have. That, in itself, has become a national disaster—many have fallen prey to painkillers and pills, and not just your "stereotypical" drug abusers. Good people from good families and those you'd never expect; no one is exempt from addiction.

In the days following my termination, there were a few damaging articles in the paper. Those articles were not tucked away in Section F but instead printed on the front page with my picture next to each one. The story was on TV that night, and people I knew from all over the state found out what was happening, prompting more calls that I didn't answer. Approximately thirty to forty unanswered calls over the next twenty-four hours kept our phone busy.

During my termination meeting, I explained to everyone present that I had used admission box cash to pay for things that suddenly came up on several occasions. It didn't happen often, but when I had to do it, I took the receipts, placed them in an envelope, put the envelope in my desk drawer for a few years, and then tossed it if nobody asked about it. That was the worst thing I did, and if I was fired for that, then so be it, but there was no way anyone could accuse me of embezzlement.

When I removed the cash for the coaches meeting supplies, I was questioned as to why I hadn't put a receipt in the cash box. I informed them that we hadn't even had the coaches meeting yet and the money hadn't been used to buy anything at that point, so I didn't have a receipt. Goodness! I removed money from the cash box, hadn't even used it, and was still fired. Being put through hell for that seemed extreme.

I admit that the process I used wasn't correct, but I did it and certainly couldn't undo it. There also wasn't any petty cash, credit card, or checkbook to use for such purposes, and requests for those things had been denied by our business manager on several occasions.

Toward the end of that meeting, the superintendent said that he was going to send an email out to all of the staff in the school district, letting them know what had occurred, but that he *would not* give a reason as to why I was being let go—a so-called "giving his word," if you will, but you've read how that goes.

It wasn't long before I received a call from the newspaper. Someone in the school was good friends with the sportswriter at the *Kalamazoo Gazette* and had forwarded him the staff email. I know who that person was, and it was disappointing to know information had been circulated without waiting to see what was really happening. The following morning, an article came out that said I had been fired because of "Financial Irregularities." So much for the superintendent not telling anyone the reason for my dismissal… another instance of him saying something and going back on his word.

Look, folks, *I didn't steal any money*, and I've had to say that to countless people along this unbelievable journey. The school's investigator only spoke with the school staff—not with me or my attorney. A conversation when things were just getting started would have taken maybe ten minutes, and none of us would be in the situation that we ended up in.

Once he was done with his investigation, my attorney got a call and told me they had me for embezzling $2,200. I got sick to my stomach.

My attorney said, "Marc, I thought they were going to say there was $30,000 to $40,000 missing."

I didn't care if I was being accused of taking twenty-two dollars. I simply couldn't believe any of it was happening. The school investigator's report was also the first time I was able to look thoroughly at the "spreadsheet" that showed the differences between my records and those of the event manager. There were several dates when she didn't have the correct starting cash amounts, used incorrect event dates, listed a middle school event as a high school event, along with a few other things that led to what could have caused some questions.

What I can tell you is that the money that was *supposed* to be turned in from those cash boxes was what I turned in, other than the times already discussed. The event manager and my secretary could have talked to me, and I would have shown them the times and documentation involved. Instead, my life was ruined.

Since my personal transition twenty-five years prior to that when I accepted Christ as my Savior, I wanted my legacy to be known as not that of a great coach, athletic director, or anything else that was "wonderful," but one of serving Him. I wanted people to know that I was a servant of Jesus, and I wanted to be known for my love of Christ. I felt that reputation and legacy were gone based on a major mistake made on behalf of the people involved.

Noah played baseball that spring, which meant I had to go to his games at the baseball field. I parked in an area close to the field, limiting the distance I had to walk to watch the game. As I arrived for the first home game of the year, Noah said that they needed someone to announce the games and that the guys on the team wanted me to do it.

Great. Just what I didn't want to do—put myself in a spot that would draw attention. The good thing was that I would be inside the press box so that nobody could see me. After three or four games, I felt like I was right at home. Around that same time, just as I was getting comfortable, the principal called me, which was surprising. He informed me that the superintendent had told him that he had to let me know he wouldn't allow me to announce the games any longer. That was such a slap in my face, and I had to tell Noah that I could no longer help out.

That one hurt. Seeing that the superintendent never came to a J.V. baseball game, someone had to have informed him I was announcing, and I'm willing to bet it was a board member I had seen there who called and questioned him about it. Since he had the authority, of course, I'm sure he thought it would be easier for him to have the principal tell me to stop announcing than doing it himself.

Finding a job was a challenge. Even though I only applied for about ten positions, I wasn't contacted about any of them. I called those places and was told that someone would get back to me if they were interested. The jobs varied, as I didn't know what I would be able to do, what I was qualified for, or who would hold the school issue against me once they Googled my name.

A couple of opportunities came my way before the incident happened but even those vanished in a hurry. Fortunately, my wife is terrific friends with a woman who was the office manager at an accounting office in Kalamazoo. They needed someone to do part-time bank reconciliations, prepare specific reports and payroll for a few businesses, and complete other tasks around the office. Diane Smith brought me on board, and I'm appreciative of that.

There I was, accused of embezzlement by the school yet hired in an accounting office. It provided some comic relief when friends asked what I was up to. I only worked fifteen to twenty hours a week while making twelve dollars an hour, but it was some much-needed income for our house, not to mention it got me out a little more. I even started talking to people again.

However, my mind began racing with all the other things that would fall prey due to the unfair accusations…

I did all the work to get our athletic Hall of Fame together, and even though it wasn't life-ending, being included based on my work at the school was still something that would have been nice. I knew then it was probably never happening. Of all the awards and honors I received over my playing and professional experiences, that one would have been the creme de la creme of them all.

My family… Perfect? None of us are. But every time I think about our kids, I am overwhelmed with who and what they are.

I could go on and on with this one, but my youngest son Noah was a sophomore in high school when my "scandal" happened and had to go to school every day and face those who accused me of doing something that I hadn't. He endured enormous pressure and some pretty hurtful remarks. Noah also suffered severe depression, but again, he is strong and endured with the help of good friends. Jarrett Miller, Christian Sanders, Hunter Erickson, Stosh Tustin, and Gavin Rogers were such a massive help to him. His basketball coach, Gary Sprague, was also instrumental in helping him cope.

My family no longer considered those people who ran the rumor mill or made accusations about me as friends, but they were respectful nonetheless because they have personalities that allow them to be that way.

The last time Noah spoke of the incident was when he happened to be walking down the hall as classes were going on. As he passed a room, he heard a student say, "I'm going to tell my dad to steal also." Noah walked into the room, right up to that person, and told him that I hadn't stolen anything, and that if he heard it again, he would take care of things differently.

Noah was 6'5" and about 210 pounds, so most people didn't want him getting angry. He'd never been in a fight up to that point, but unfortunately, we weren't out of the woods yet. During the passing time between classes, Noah went back to the classroom and apologized to the teacher whose class he'd interrupted. The teacher responded by saying, "Noah, you don't have to apologize. You didn't do anything wrong, and I understand."

We were appreciative of that teacher's understanding and happy about how some of the others at school watched over Noah during what could have been a time when a kid loses it. As it turned out, that boy who made the comment later approached Noah and apologized. Noah hugged him and said, "It's over." Even with that, he should never have been forced into that situation.

My other kids were older and had plenty of friends. They hadn't heard from anyone who believed the school's side, and most were supportive of our family. To this day, none of my children are happy with those who were involved in the ugly accusation. I've asked them to forgive, as I have.

It takes time, but I got it done with the Big Guy in front of me the entire time. Even though forgiveness is commanded, I still ask God for strength in that area. There are indeed times when my mind wants to wander into dark areas because, although I've forgiven, I haven't forgotten. My kids aren't ready to forgive the school's leadership, but I know, one day, they will.

31

4TH OF JULY

W hen Josh met Morgan, we thought he couldn't have picked a better lifemate. It was about a twelve-hour drive from Michigan to where he was living, so far and few between were the times we saw him. But on the 4th of July the same year I was fired, we made the trip to Suwannee, Georgia to see him for a long weekend and spend time with our son and Morgan's family.

That trip also gave us a chance to get out of town, which we had not had the opportunity to do since my crime of the century. We didn't know Morgan's family all that well but had enjoyed meeting them the prior fall before when they treated us to the Alabama vs. West Virginia football game at the Georgia Dome in Atlanta.

We arrived two days before the 4th and had a lovely first night, but then we were told that we'd get up fairly early and head off to the lake for a couple of days with friends of theirs. I felt awful at the outset, thinking that maybe we'd inconvenienced their plans. They reassured us that we weren't in the way and that there was plenty of room for everyone at their friends' lake house. In fact, their friends were planning on having us. So, when in Rome...

We made the hour trip up to Lake Burton in northern Georgia

and arrived to find about twenty-five people at the house for the country's celebration. It was a beautiful place. Eric, the owner, walked us to the end of the dock, pointed at a massive home across the water, and told us it was Nick Saban's lake home. Us being huge Alabama fans, we were in awe. He pointed at another house and told us it was country music star Alan Jackson's lake home.

Two things: It was awe-inspiring. Also, Marc and Peg were way out of their league.

The following day, Morgan's dad Jay, me, Josh, and Eric went four-wheeling in two Razer off-road vehicles. Josh and Jay were in one, Eric and I in another. We took off like bats out of heck, down a paved road for a while before veering off onto some dirt roads. Eric took a quick right turn where there was no road at all. I'd never done such a thing before, so I was having a ton of fun. As we roared up a hill, we hit rocks and many other obstacles and the wheel turned sideways, causing a broken tie rod. There was no way to steer.

Josh and Jay had to make the half-hour trip back to the house to get a truck and trailer while Eric and I stayed with our vehicle in the middle of nowhere. Eric said he never went up in that area without some sort of weapon because of bears, mountain lions, and other predators, but primarily because of people you might run into. He then told me the movie *Deliverance* was filmed a short distance from where we were! Yikes.

Thank goodness he had his weapons, right? Just as I was ready to exhale a sigh of relief, Eric said, "Marc, the only bad thing is that the weapons are in the other Razer, so we don't have them." Uh-oh.

After about an hour, Jay returned with the truck and trailer. We hauled the beat-up Razer down the hill and loaded it onto the trailer. There were a few noises in the woods, but we didn't see any danger. At least we had the guns by our sides.

We took the broken buggy to the marina at the lake. Welding would only provide a temporary fix. A new tie rod was needed, so the marina gave us directions to a place called Mike's Bikes. We loaded up and made the twenty-minute drive to another middle of nowhere spot.

Eric walked up to a giant garage and knocked, but nobody answered. I mean, it was the 4th of July, after all, and I was sure it was closed. A minute later, a guy who was about five feet tall and four feet wide with the bushiest mustache I've ever seen walked over from a nearby house and told us in a deep southern drawl that he'd gotten a call that we might be coming by. Thank goodness. At least there was phone reception!

He looked at the busted machine and confirmed we needed a tie rod but recommended we replace both of them. So, we went into a building that looked like an *American Pickers* stop, stepped over a half dozen boxes, and he pulled one box out from the rubble. The garage had no rhyme nor reason to its organizational structure except to him; and sure enough, that box contained the two tie rods we needed.

He put on the tie rods and said, "These are kind of expensive, so it'll be eighty dollars total."

Eric pulled out his wad of cash, ripped off a $100 bill, and said, "Keep the change."

"Mike" asked if we were sure, and Eric said, "Absolutely." He'd helped us on the 4th of July, and the repair really wasn't all that expensive.

As we loaded back up, we discovered a missing rear light. "Mike" had one of those also, so we headed back to the garage, meandering our way through the heaps of crap where he picked out a small box. What do you know! A taillight. We asked how much and without hesitation, he answered, "A hundred dollars!"

Ol' Mike lived in the backwoods, but he was no dummy.

Before we left, he asked Eric what he did for work, and Eric casually said he did construction work. Little did the guy know that Eric's company built Atlanta's Mercedes Benz Stadium and the well-known Georgia Aquarium. Just a tiny little company. Right!

I was impressed, but not "Mike." He shrugged and asked what Jay did, and Jay answered he was in transportation. His family has a massive logistics company—not quite a dinky delivery company. Still, Mike was uninspired.

When he asked me, I said I was a retired teacher. Mike perked up. He proudly said in his deep, southern accent, "Hey, my daughter is a teacher! She teaches them 'R' kids."

I won't use the word, but it was *that* R-word. Keep in mind that both Jay and Eric have kids with special needs. I hid my head, obviously embarrassed, but Mike never thought anything about it, choosing to continue the conversation.

Next, he asked Eric if he ever raced his machines, and Eric said that there was a place about twenty minutes away. Mike knew the location, but said, "Twenty minutes? I can get there in about ten, but I have to drive through N-town to get there."

What?! Yes, he'd spouted *that* nasty word, once again saying something that made us all cringe.

We were vacationing with probably a half-dozen African American kids, so we were more than a little caught off guard and disgusted. That guy probably hadn't been more than a half-hour away from his house in his entire life and thought that was "the way it was"—the ancient south.

It was about 4:00 in the afternoon and we hadn't enjoyed any lake time yet. Eric apologized for everything and felt bad about not being at the lake on such a gorgeous day, but I told him it was probably the best 4th I'd ever had. What an experience that made for a great tale and valuable lesson. I'll carry that one in my hip pocket forever.

BACK TO THE GRIND

In July 2015, after our trip, I received a call from my attorney. He explained that the Kalamazoo County Sheriff had completed their four-month and much more thorough investigation of my school incident. They'd talked to everyone involved, plus my attorney. I wanted to tell my story so badly, but Jim Shinar said that I was paying him to be my voice. I understood and even appreciated that, although I would have liked to have been the one to tell the story.

During that phone call from Jim, he informed me that the Sheriff couldn't find evidence of me stealing money. They could only take a $200 misdemeanor charge to the prosecutor's office for the money I'd admitted taking—the funds I'd planned on using for the coaches meeting... funds that *had been returned*, as I never had a chance to spend them.

It's disappointing and almost laughable that the detective called the school to relay those findings and our superintendent still wanted him to take the misdemeanor charge downtown, again for money that wasn't actually missing or stolen. Geesh!

The prosecutor's office looked at the evidence and didn't support the $200 charge. Peg and I were ecstatic. We thanked him for the call, and then we went outside and took a walk around our neighborhood like we had done numerous times in the past. That walk was our first of the summer. I'd been so uncomfortable with going out in public and seeing anyone. Even doing something mundane like taking a walk bothered me.

At that point, I thought about the nightmare I'd had for the last five months and how it had all happened. I figured everything would go back to normal, but that certainly wasn't the case. My depression and fear of going out in public were still very real, and I knew that the entire issue was far from over.

As is usually the case in the press, an article was published with the results of the investigation, but it was hidden in the sports section, not on the front page like the prior articles in which I'd been accused. There was nothing on the television news, as had been the case when the "story" first came out. Not nearly as many people found out the result as what had heard the initial report. The media in our country is pathetic, and that was another case of only wanting to sensationalize a story instead of being fair.

Because of that, I wanted the school to issue a public apology and request that it be on the paper's front page and ask that the local television station make an announcement. The intent was not to punish the school or to have them knock on my door with a half-hearted "sorry," but to restore my reputation. I wanted people to see that the entire issue wasn't what it appeared to be, and the perception that so many probably had could be changed.

It didn't matter if it was written in the sky every day. There would still be some that would believe I was guilty. However, I needed closure.

My attorney drafted a letter to the school's attorney and requested an apology. About a week later, we received a response indicating in an unyielding tone that they would in no way apologize, and they also told us that filing a lawsuit would be ludicrous. That irked me, so Peg and I decided to ask Jim to start the process of a suit, for, among other things, slander and libel.

There was no intent to chastise or punish them but to help my cause. We had also sustained a financial blow. I didn't receive payment from the school from the time I was fired. We had to pay our legal fees, which I had zero problems doing because of Jim Shinar's great work, and we had to take out around $50,000 of our retirement savings to cover costs, including college tuition. Peg and I were unsure where we live, so after a while, I thought a fresh start might be a good thing.

It was always our plan to work, live, retire, die, and be buried in Richland, Michigan. But nothing was the same, and I still felt embarrassed about having my name dragged through the mud. Kelli and Trevor lived five minutes away on Gull Lake, and Marc and Lyndsie were about fifteen minutes away with our granddaughters. Josh was living in Athens, Georgia, getting his Master's degree at the University of Georgia with his fiancé, Morgan, who had opened a brand new clothing store. Noah was planning on attending the University of Alabama. We knew we wanted to be near family, but we were confused about what to do.

33

NOW WHAT DO I DO?

As we began a new chapter in the remarkable and joyful circumstance (yes, I'm kidding), more stressful situations were bound to be ahead. We could have dropped the need for amends and moved on, but my name and future needed repair and restoration.

I know you're wondering how much we sued for, right? It may be hard to believe, but never during the entire time of setting up the lawsuit did my attorney and I talk numbers. The dollar amount wasn't discussed until much later. That being said, we also knew the financial end was vital; as I said, we had to take out a lot of our retirement money, lost the wages I would have been paid if I hadn't been needlessly fired, and the inability to find that second career I was hoping to have wouldn't have existed. However, I told Jim that the first priority of the lawsuit was receiving an apology.

Once the paperwork was drawn up, a period of taking depositions began. I didn't even know what a deposition was until I was educated about what it entailed. It was then determined which individuals would be named in the lawsuit. They were people that at one point I'd considered close confidantes and allies.

I could barely sleep the night before each individual was

deposed and we got their statements. It wasn't that bad once we got started, with the exception of sitting there with each person, knowing what they'd meant to me in the past compared to what they meant to me at that moment. A few of them had been excellent friends but had somehow morphed into just people I was suing.

Each of the depositions lasted an hour or two, with my attorney questioning each person. Later in the spring, the school's side stated that they wanted to depose me. I went in, and it was apparent that their attorney was trying to wear me down in an attempt to make me say something or admit guilt, which, of course, wasn't going to happen. My deposition started at 9:00 that morning and finished around 4:30 that afternoon. Talk about a long day! There were two times on the way home that I was stopped at a red light and when it turned green, the person behind me had to beep their horn so that I would drive. I was so mentally drained that it was hard to even concentrate.

Soon after my deposition was over, the school's attorney called and said they wanted to settle the matter. Since there was no apology on the table and the dollar amount they offered was ridiculous, we were quick to decline. A second offer came later, and though it was much more, there was still no apology, and the amount wasn't close to what we'd lost. It was evident to me and my attorney that the school knew there was a problem and they wanted to wrap things up before having to spend an enormous dollar amount.

During the lawsuit process, the school claimed they had Governmental Immunity and we couldn't sue them. I'd never heard of that before and figured it was a desperate attempt by the school to get us to drop the suit. They filed paperwork that requested the suit be dismissed based on that "immunity" thing.

I couldn't believe that the school might be getting away with discrediting my name due to a completely false accusation of embezzling money. It's wrong, but anger began boiling up inside of me, and I had to talk to the Lord a great deal about it and ask Him to remove that anger from my thoughts.

In the summer of 2016, we finally had a hearing in court where the school's attorney argued their side, and my attorney argued why our case shouldn't be ignored. My family was there with me, which was huge from a morale standpoint. Their presence also allowed everyone there to know they were standing with me.

The judge's final decision was that the school was to be given Governmental Immunity. Although I was never charged with anything, I also never received a formal apology and still haven't to this day.

When it was all over and we left the courtroom, I couldn't have been happier with how Jim performed and the legal arguments he presented. I don't think the school's attorney looked as confident as Jim. Their attorney was a good guy; probably the kind of man I'd enjoy playing golf and having fun with. In fact, I still feel the same way about him even now.

I understand that school employees should be given protection from disciplinary issues that come along. Still, I cannot figure out how ruining someone's name and reputation occurs when a school's statements are false. Regardless, I do want to state that I do not believe there was an intention to make my life awful, but huge mistakes in how things were handled were definitely made by some good people. I still wish I could have gotten an "I'm sorry" along the way.

The entire experience was total misery, but I'm sure it was unpleasant for them as well.

34

LESSONS LEARNED

Adversity will always come your way if you have even one characteristic that qualifies you for such situations. But you can breathe! When things happen that you don't necessarily want to invade your life, stress and anxiety will fill the mind and heart. A feeling in your stomach as if you've just been punched occurs, and there are usually only two things that can make that awful feeling go away. Those things are time and a healthy relationship with Christ.

During my experience, I went to God and asked Him to guide and protect me from any evil that might come my way. There is absolutely no doubt in my mind that He did just that.

Some might say, "Well, if He cared about you, He wouldn't have let you go through that nasty experience in the first place." To that I say, if you genuinely love God and put your trust in Him, His word guarantees that you will indeed suffer and feel pain at some point in your life.

I started reading the book of Job the same night I was fired. Talk about suffering and adversity! This guy lost it all—his wife, children, home, land, and everything he had! Everything *except* his faith in

God. In the end, he gained more than he initially had, but during that awful experience, his life was almost unbearable.

The phrase "what doesn't kill you makes you stronger" is Biblical in a sense.

It says in the New International Version of **ROMANS 5:3**,

> *"Not only so, but we also glory in our sufferings, because we know that suffering produces perseverance; perseverance, character; and character, hope."*

We are to *glory* in our sufferings... but, man, it sure is hard to do when you're in the midst of the fire. It may sound crazy, but there is an answer for everything in the Bible if you just look for it!

You will also learn who your real friends are and those that truly care about you. With something as traumatic as I went through, many times, people don't know what to do or say. I get it. However, support is so crucial to the ones who need it. Please don't forget that.

"True friends." That's a phrase that can be overused, and one you may think is accurate until someone doesn't need you anymore or is too afraid to get involved. During my entire career as a coach and A.D., some people warmed up to me, did nice things for us, and made my family believe that their friendship was unbreakable... right up until their child graduated or stopped playing sports. I cannot begin to tell you how many folks like that crossed our path. We thought the friendship was genuine, only to see a fast departure when they didn't need us as "friends" any longer. Not everyone was in that camp, but many were.

In the first few days, many individuals dropped me words of encouragement through texts, cards, emails, and other forms of communication. It was hard to face the suffering, but I was encouraged by those who made their journeys to my home at a time I needed them the most. Larry Wallace, Mike Sanders, Joe Peters, Mike Foster, Pastor Bryan Tema, and others were at my door in the early stages, and I know that had to be tough for them. But, man, did I appreciate that.

Another couple, Scott and Dee Latt, called and *told* us they were coming over one Saturday night. They wouldn't have it any other way. They knew that Saturday was the night of the All-Sports Boosters major fundraiser I had worked so hard on getting people to attend over the years. I wasn't going, and the Latts knew. Instead of attending, they came and helped us try to recover by showing their support. The following fall, when the first Friday night football game took place, Scott and Dee came over again, as they knew I would be having a tough time since I couldn't go to the game. *That* is friendship!

You'll also learn who never were your supporters. The biggest disappointment for me was that our Sports Boosters never attempted to say thank you for what had been done over the twenty-eight years I worked at the school. There were a few individuals who sent words of encouragement, but that group as a whole didn't say boo.

They weren't the only ones. People with whom I'd regularly talked to, worked with at events, and had what I thought were great relationships with, ignored me. That sounds brutal, I know. I also understand that some might not have wanted to get involved or even didn't know what to do. After all, I essentially blew everybody off the first few days. It was just a tough time for many, I'm sure.

I feel that there were some people who looked at me more so for the "role" I had at the school. It was that role they'd warmed up to, not me as a person, and the realization hurt. Me no longer being in that role made it easier for them to shut me out as a person. Going to Noah's basketball games and seeing some of those people made me sick. It wasn't an angry sick. I just knew that for them, ignoring me or not saying anything—not even a "hi" or passing head nod—wasn't a big deal.

One person, Dave Adamski, came over at the first event I went to and said, "Marc Throop, you're a good man. Don't let anybody ever tell you differently." That meant a lot. Ken Fouts, who I had only rarely spoken with, also came and sat with me at a couple of games. What great comfort that was from people with whom I'd never had much interaction.

We would be wise to consider these words spoken by Jesus to His disciples, bearing in mind that we *will* have tribulation, trials, difficulties, opposition, sorrow, and sometimes even depression in this life. We will have false accusations, even slander, yet we can be of good cheer because of the promise of God that no matter how dark the days may become, we *are* going to make it to the finish line.

Remember, as we're told in **ISAIAH, CHAPTER 40**, Jesus has already won the victory for us! (Isaiah 40).

Some people are so focused on their pain that they can't see the greatness on the other side. Easier said than done, I know, but you *must* know that it's what is promised to you by Him.

TRUST HIM WHEN YOU ARE SUFFERING.

He certainly doesn't answer your email, but He does answer your "knee" mail.

35

FINAL YEAR IN RICHLAND

The fall of 2016 was another tough beginning of the school year, but things were starting to get a little better. The times of flat-out depression and anxiety surrounding our family's plight seemed to lessen as we looked forward to Noah's senior year in high school. We believed that it would bring to a close our thirty years in Gull Lake, even though it wasn't ending like we always thought it would.

Noah got a scholarship to Alabama, but even with our income, it wasn't enough for him to attend. He also became the leader of the school's spirited student section at football games. Noah was working harder than ever at getting better both physically and academically in order to achieve some of his post-high school goals.

We also learned that Marc and Lyndsie were expecting their third child, which excited us to no end. We felt so blessed that his family lived close to us and that we could see the girls so often. Natalie usually spent a night with us on the weekend, whereas Annie went to her dad's. She was around less, but we still saw her a good bit. Their family was doing well, and Marc provided for them while Lyndsie juggled everything in the house. We knew that if we moved, leaving them would be hard, but they were settled and doing great.

Marc is the hardest working person I know. Lyndsie is a great mom, and we see the kids benefiting greatly from her being at home a lot while also working her job.

Kelli and Trevor continued to do well in their professions, so there was no need to worry about them. They lived on Gull Lake, and Trevor was doing exceptionally well in selling boats. Starting a family of their own wasn't happening as quickly as Peg and I were hoping, but that was their decision. Kelli started a new business out of their home, a company that Trevor's grandfather had done for many years—the trophy and award business. As only Kelli could, she came up with a business name that fit her to a tee: Trophy Wife Awards! That has become a bustling operation for her, which is no surprise, as she is astute, hardworking, and personable.

Josh and Morgan continued their lives down south in Athens, Georgia. Josh began his Master's program in accounting, and Morgan started her new business, the clothing store in Athens called The Indigo Child. Remember? I described it as a "high-end hippy boutique" earlier. Peg, Noah, and I took a quick weekend trip in November 2016 to see them and the store, and it really is a neat place. We are proud of them for how they've proceeded after graduating from Alabama, but we are so proud of all of our kids for how they've turned out.

But, Peg and I knew we needed to decide where living might be best for us, and we took many things into consideration. Still, leaving Gull Lake seemed best for a variety of reasons, and as the fall concluded, we tried to prepare ourselves.

Basketball season was about to start for Noah, and the thought of having to go up to school was not overly exciting to me. That feeling hit me full force at the annual Parent Information Night for winter sports, where the athletic director talked about important information parents needed to know and coaches introduced their teams. Seeing the two people who initiated my problems there made me want to throw up, but I also looked at the program's setup that night with pride, knowing I was the one who started it.

I couldn't help but gaze at the championship banners hanging on the gym walls. I had ordered them when the high school was built, and seeing all those championship teams from when I was the athletic director reminded me of happy days. However, one thing was glaringly missing from those banners, and that was the fact that no other championship banners had shown up since I'd left as the A.D. I know there had to have been some teams that won titles since I'd left, but the banners hadn't been updated so that people coming into the gym could see them. That's another "oh, well" since I wasn't in charge any longer, but the banners having not been updated still bothered me.

While I sat there that night, I paid each banner a little extra attention. They are organized so that each of the varsity teams has one that displays the years they won a conference championship, district championship, regional championship, and advancement into the state tournament. I never kept track before, but I made my best effort to count the number of titles our coaches and kids had won. I found that during my twenty years as the A.D., there were 101 conference titles, forty-three district, thirty-six regional, and sixty-four trips to the state finals by a team or individual.

An awful feeling began tearing me apart emotionally, and it lasted when we got home. Post Traumatic Stress Disorder was acting up again and reminding me of the unjust experience we'd gone through. However, I finally settled down late that night. I was humbled in knowing that Christ went through a whole lot more than I did, and He did that for me!

Peg was becoming more and more limited in what she was able to do and how she felt. It was noticeable to people when they watched her walk or move. She was still working at Taste of Heaven, but those days were numbered. She was scheduled to have back surgery in December, but she wanted to make sure she got through the Christmas season. When she'd get home from work, I helped her inside and moved her to a comfortable position. I hated seeing the pain that made her cry from doing even simple tasks like getting into bed.

When my kids were around, especially Noah at night, I tried to be an example of what staying strong during a tough time looked like. Kelli and Noah were probably the two that helped most with tasks and errands. They knew their mom, who was always active, never sat down, and constantly found something to do to stay busy and on her feet, needed help she'd never ask for. Marc and Josh were concerned, but Josh was thirteen hours away and Marc had his own family and worked a ton.

Peg's mobility and pain also caused her limited time to have her granddaughters spend the night with us. If they were to come over, she would undoubtedly have tried to push herself to be a part of their being there, so I had to tell Marc that having them for the night probably wasn't going to work until after her back surgery. That was heartbreaking for both him and me.

The kids always showed strength around Peg, as they knew that her seeing them downtrodden in some sort of state of depression certainly wouldn't help. I did a lot more laundry, housecleaning, dishwashing, and taking care of the daily chores. I didn't want her to have to do it. Peg made it a whole lot easier on all of us with her outlook and attitude.

She always did everything around the house. Peg never thought twice about it when she did "mom" or "wife" tasks. Once she went to bed at night and Noah did his studying, I made my way into the living room to watch a game or relax, but most nights, I cried. Seeing what was happening—my wife slowing down substantially and my life turned completely around by the circumstances we had to deal with for a couple of years—burdened me yet again. Selfish! That's what that was, and I just wanted to be able to shake it.

Peg had issues, people we knew were going through difficulties with their health, and watching our country go through some callous times was hard. Life wasn't happening the way I had intended it to go once I had retired from working. With that, I knew deep down that I had much to be thankful for, and I expressed that to others when I could. Having the presence of the Holy Spirit moving us along and reminding us that what He had done certainly allowed us to have some great days as well.

It probably sounds like it was a "woe is me" life most of the time, but I was grateful for what I had, especially my family. They mean everything to me.

Noah and I were excited about how the college football season had gone. Our new favorite team, the Alabama Crimson Tide, went through an undefeated season and was the first-ranked team in the nation. However, watching my alma mater, Western Michigan University, also go through an undefeated season was surprising to most people. It lit the Kalamazoo community on fire.

Some of my former teammates from Western and I said to each other, "Just imagine if social media had been around back when we had our magical season and were ranked tenth in the country." Our basketball and football teams from that year were, without question, two groups, along with the 1983 volleyball season, that gave more excitement to WMU and the community than any other in the school's history. It certainly was fun to be a Bronco and watch the team do so well.

I only went to one Western Michigan home game all year, whereas I was used to going to several. I was still uneasy about going out in public. Sad, but that was my fault. I had no reason to feel bad, but I couldn't completely shake the anxiety.

Many members of our 1976 basketball team happened to be in town for a reunion. As a kind gesture, WMU Athletic Director Kathy Beauregard provided us with tickets to that game at Westerns Waldo Stadium, and it was funny that in a stadium of 30,000 seats, ours was right next to my attorney. That was fun, as we had a chance to enjoy him socially. When he was a kid, Jim was a big fan of our basketball team, so I know he enjoyed it as well.

As we walked back to our cars in a parking lot across the street, I noticed a man staring in our direction. He came right up to me and asked if my name was Marc Throop. When I nervously affirmed who I was, he introduced himself as the detective who had handled my case with the school. I wanted to hug him but settled for a handshake instead.

He said, "Marc, I just wanted to say I'm sorry for what the school put you through. Keep your head up."

Finally, someone apologized! That felt good, and the rest of the day was even more enjoyable. The guys came to our house that night for a party, making the entire day a total success.

Isn't it amazing what a little encouragement can do to brighten the day and allow you to feel good about yourself? A lot more of that should happen, especially with the way the world is now.

Noah's high school basketball season finally kicked off, and it was amazing to see what that kid had gone through to get where he was. As a young boy in elementary and middle school, and even his first couple of years of high school, if someone would have said that he was going to be the captain and a starter for the basketball team, I would have recommended a good psychiatrist, but Noah accomplished both feats.

MORE "FUN"

On December 9th, I felt a little poke in my back but figured it was just another sign of being sixty. However, it continued throughout the day, and I thought maybe I'd stop in and get it checked out. At 4:45, I arrived at the ER, and they immediately brought me in for an EKG. When that test turned out fine, I was told to wait in the lobby. Little did I know I'd wait for nearly two hours while my breathing continued to get worse.

I finally got into an ER room and waited another forty-five minutes until I saw another person. Blood work was done, and after another two hours, it came back a little goofy and I went in for a CT scan. Another half-hour in, and a doctor told me that he had some bad news. I had several blood clots in my lung, a pulmonary embolism, which, if not treated quickly, could kill me. Okay!

When the doctor asked us if I wanted to be resuscitated if my heart stopped, Peg and I looked at each other. With a straight face, she said, "He's well insured, so can I have a minute to think about it?" We both laughed, but nobody else did.

They got moving pretty quickly at that point, and I was admitted into the hospital and had a delightful (note my sarcasm) two-day stay. I couldn't breathe well, but at least my diagnosis was known and I could start treatment. I was admitted on Thursday, and on Friday morning, the nurse said, "Well, we sure are glad you're still with us today." I was kind of happy about that as well.

I was somewhat limited in what I could do physically, but thank goodness for Peg and my sons, Marc and Noah, and my daughter, Kelli. There was lots of support and care, but we were all awaiting the upcoming week. Peg would finally be going under the knife for back surgery.

That day came, and we were almost as excited as we would be if we were going on vacation. However, the event didn't come without a bit of anxiety. Around 1:00 in the morning, I saw headlights pull into the driveway. As I went to look out the window, I heard banging and became nervous. I immediately grabbed my Smith & Wesson 357 handgun and went to the front room. I opened the door and saw my son Josh, who surprised us by flying in for the weekend to be with us during Peg's surgery. That boy is lucky to be alive!

After sitting up until around 2:30, talking with him and Noah, who had also gotten up, we finally went to bed. It was a school night, so Noah being up at 2:30 in the morning wasn't ideal, but the weather was terrible, and him not having school the next day was a good bet. Plus, his idol was home from Georgia. Prayers were answered within a few hours! No school.

The morning came, and we all made the journey with Peg to the hospital for her to have her surgery. It started at 11:30, and the doctor came out around 2:00 and told us that everything went as well as it possibly could have gone. We finally got to see her around 3:30.

Peg was with a physical therapist who had her on her feet for a short walk. We were all thrilled. No more leg or back pain, and she was able to stand upright without slouching. We gave thanks to Him for allowing things to happen and having Dr. Brombley perform the surgery without complication.

It was time to begin a new phase of our lives, especially after the challenges we'd faced over the past two years. So much agony, discomfort, and lack of mobility were over for my wife. It was more than we could have possibly hoped for. Even though the Parkinson's was still there, Peg was ready to lead an everyday life again.

Noah's final basketball season was a lot of fun for us, even though we only won eight games. We were cautious when his team lost or Noah didn't play as much as he would have liked, but he had Gary Sprague as his coach, who knew what Noah had gone through between my school ordeal and my wife's health. Gary encouraged Noah, and we felt fortunate to have him with our son.

For the second straight season, Noah was named as having the Best Team Attitude. Players vote on that, so it made it even more special. He loved his teammates despite not having a lot of team success. That winter also saw Peg moving much better and without pain. She felt great and was not in excruciating pain. Things seemed to be turning for us.

Winter was coming to a close. Going to Gull Lake events and seeing the people who had taken so much from my life still wasn't much fun. Peg and I still were trying to figure out where our future would lead us. We knew Gull Lake was probably not going to be where we lived, but where in the world God would send us was still unknown.

However, another positive thing happened in January…

I was convinced by a couple of people—my kids—to become an Uber driver. I laughed at the suggestion, but knew some income had to start flowing. And so, I began my driving career.

Believe it or not, I made decent money and had a ton of fun at the same time. It's certainly not for everyone, but I enjoyed driving and talking with people. I wasn't changing the world, but I also wasn't looking to be "the boss" anymore, and that was a great feeling.

Witnessing to others about God's greatness and getting back out in public without anxiety were both things that were important to me. I saw that the strength I was receiving could only be coming from one place.

"Live by the truth of God's Word, which encourages you to be strong and courageous! Do not be afraid and do not panic… For the Lord your God will personally go ahead of you. He will neither fail you nor abandon you."

— DEUT. 31:6 NLT

37

SPRING OF 2017

Noah started his final season as a high school baseball player, and it was the last season we would experience with our kids participating in sports.

Emotions race through your mind during that time, and you reminisce about all the events, practices, coaching, and everything else you've done with your kids. Every instance of our firstborn Marc playing in his first youth basketball game up until that last season with Noah ran through my mind. Instead of feeling joy and excitement about everything we'd been through, I couldn't wait until it was all over and I'd no longer have anything to do with Gull Lake. It shouldn't have been that way.

Noah's baseball season was anticipated to be a great one for him and his team. The expectations for our guys were high with all of the talent we had. However, expectations and outcomes don't always match up like you want them to. The final record of the team that year was 19 and 19—a huge disappointment.

A new coach at the varsity level for the first time can make that happen; he's trying to do things his way when kids are used to dealing with the previous coach. Folks, only nine guys can play at a time, and when you have an excess of twenty players on the team, it's bound to cause some unhappy campers. That's what happened. Kids complained a lot, both those who played and those that didn't. Same for the parents.

Several freshmen and sophomore players were brought up to play instead of the upperclassmen. A couple deserved to play, but a few didn't perform so well. It's hard for a coach to make those decisions, and when the younger kids don't perform any better than the older kids, it has all the makings for a rough year.

Indeed it was. Some kids and parents didn't even come to the end-of-the-season awards program, which I don't think was the right thing to do, but it happened. I had questions about how things happened during the year, but for Noah's sake, we never considered not attending. The coach was putting his footprint on the program and making the decisions he needed to make. A good guy, a good coach; he had a bright future. Noah wound up playing quite a bit, but others didn't.

We only had two more events at the school where I would see "those people." The first was the senior awards program that was held at our church. I had verbal contact with a couple of people who made decisions during my tough time. Both were pleasant, but the uncomfortable feeling was enormous. That was the last time I spoke with them. Noah got a couple of awards that we were proud of him for, but it was a "let's get this over with" night for all of us.

The last event was graduation at Miller Auditorium on the Western Michigan campus. That's always a nice night for kids and parents. The facility is beautiful, and it makes for a memorable evening for everyone. All of our kids were there, along with our son-in-law, our daughter-in-law, and Josh's fiancé, making it even more special for Noah.

Once I got in the car after it was over, I was overcome with emotion and broke down crying. Not because my last child was graduating, but because of how things ended for me and the disrespect the school had for my entire family. Again, what a selfish deal on my part. It was time to celebrate!

Peg and I had a major decision to make in regards to our future, and it was time to make it. Noah had already decided that he would attend the University of Alabama, so his journey south would begin as had Josh's. The big issue was that there was no way possible to afford to send him there. Our financial earnings weren't quite what they had been at one time. I had not seriously worked for two years, so it was time to get creative and make some out-of-the-box decisions.

And so, we decided we would move to Alabama!

Having lived in Michigan all my life, making that decision seemed like a dream... or more closely, a nightmare. We kept our house in Michigan to rent and found a place that June in Northport, Alabama, about ten minutes from the University of Alabama. I couldn't believe we were going to make a change of that magnitude, which was such a long way from "home."

For the month and a half before the move, I agonized with the thought of moving. I always believed that I would work, retire, live, and be buried in Richland, Michigan. Those plans changed back on February 25, 2015, but the main reason we wanted to move was to get Noah to college. Being retired meant we were able to pack up and leave.

On July 30, our daughter Kelli threw us a going-away party. We had a great turnout, but we were also sad knowing we were leaving the next morning. It was hard to get the word out to everyone we wanted to see, but well over 100 people showed up to say *adios*.

It was also the last night we would sleep in our house of twenty-five years. Lots of crying took place that night. Kids' birthday parties, nearly three decades of Christmas and other holidays with our family, and too many other events in our home tore me apart, along with the thought of making the trip the next day. As I told many people, we didn't want to move, but we couldn't wait to leave.

On July 31, my birthday, I got in the truck we'd packed the previous day, Peg got in our car, and we were off to Alabama.

It took me twenty minutes to stop weeping, but we had indeed prayed a great deal about the whole thing before making the final decision to move. I trusted what God was doing and the plans He had for us. We got about ten of the twelve driving hours out of the way and stopped for the night. We then finished up the drive the following day and arrived at our new living quarters.

Peg and I moved into Forest Trail Apartments, which was a nice place. We overlooked a beautiful pool and manicured grounds. The quality of life we experienced made things a little easier.

That first day, we got in the pool and scratched our heads, wondering if we were dreaming. We laughed about the fact that we felt like we were on vacation at a resort. It wasn't as nice as that, really, but we weren't used to lying back and relaxing. After a week, Peg jokingly asked when our vacation was over and if it was time to go back home. Things were turning out fine for us, but we missed friends, our kids, grandkids, our house, and most everything else.

Moving to Alabama accomplished a couple of things:

- We got out of town. We, especially me, were no longer happy there.
- One of us getting a full-time job allowed us to get in-state tuition for Noah, and we saved thousands of dollars in college expenses. As she was feeling pretty good, we decided Peg would find full-time employment since I was starting to make decent money driving Uber and the university did not consider that a full-time job. She got a job working at Great American Cookie. Right up her alley. We knew she couldn't do it forever because of Parkinson's issues, but for the time being, it was perfect.

We fell into things and adjusted pretty well. While one of the maintenance guys at our complex was up at our place, we talked about Alabama football, which wasn't unusual; *everybody* there talks about it. He told us he had season tickets and that he knew someone in Tennessee looking to unload a couple. The price was right, so we grabbed them. We loved going to those games and tailgating on the quad. I've been to games at huge football schools like Michigan, Michigan State, and Notre Dame, but never have I experienced an environment like that.

The funny thing is, God's plans for you happen in crazy ways.

Had it not been for what happened to me at Gull Lake, we may never have moved and Noah would not have gone to Alabama. Even though he had a scholarship, it wasn't enough to cover everything. God made a way, as He always does.

Our new friend, Russell Estes, the maintenance guy that helped get us the Alabama football tickets, was more helpful than we could have imagined. He recommended a church for us, a place to get our car fixed, and just about anything else we needed. He was the dictionary definition and Biblical example of an angel —yet another of God's examples of providing what we needed. I'm sure God probably laughed at us and said, "You must remember that I will take care of you, and remember that My plans are perfect."

Well, we had officially moved from Michigan to Alabama. Never in a million years would I have ever thought that would happen, but we made the move, and, as I said, we often felt like we were on vacation. Of course, reality eventually began to set in, and we started our "normal" life.

The good thing was that nobody knew or gave a hoot who Marc Throop was. The bad news? Nobody cared or gave a hoot who Marc Throop was. Peg and I were always so used to being "out there" and trying to help and do the right thing for others. Now we were just two faces in the crowd that needed a long time to trust and build reputations in a new community.

We were concerned about how Noah would feel about us being so close, but if he wanted to go to Alabama, it was a sacrifice he knew he had to make. Right! We saw him more than we thought we would, and it was by his choosing. Of course, many of those calls were to know if we wanted to take him out to eat. Imagine that.

With things going so well for us, our efforts were turned to Josh and Morgan's upcoming wedding. When the happy day came, it was nothing short of phenomenal. Jay and Dawn Carr threw a wedding for the ages, and the entire weekend was a party.

The wedding was on Thanksgiving weekend, so they had dinner at their home in the beautiful River Club community in Suwanee, Georgia. It was a large home, which was a good thing. Over seventy-five people showed up for Thanksgiving dinner due to a lot of family being in town for the wedding.

My brother, Peg's siblings and their kids were there, along with Morgan's side of her family. Guess what? Everybody got along! It's miraculous considering the eclectic mix of people. Liberal, conservative, gay, straight, and even someone from Ukraine were all under one roof, enjoying one another's company. The only argument that day was when someone rooted against the Detroit Lions. Those were almost fighting words. Thankfully, no one cared much for talking about taboo subjects.

The rehearsal dinner took place the next night, and over 100 people attended. We had a great meal, and the fellowship was perfect. The only glitch in the night was when I went to pay. My credit card was declined. Uh-oh! Peg got on the horn with the company, and they denied it only because it was such a large amount. I looked at Jay Carr—Morgan's dad—and said, "Don't leave yet." It was actually kind of funny.

The wedding had everything you could ask. Over 400 people attended, and there was an unlimited amount of food and beverages, a station where someone made hand-rolled cigars, and a ton of other things that made it a celebration like no other. It was indeed a party to the moon. In fact, that was the name of the band that played, and that put the night over the top. They'd played at President Obama's Inauguration Ball and also at President Trump's New Year's Eve parties. Watching everyone have so much fun was incredible.

Before the wedding, my attorney notified me that everything was officially over, but I wasn't too happy that the school never made an apology. I couldn't believe the statements claiming that I was a thief and a liar were never going to see rectification and that those at school were going to get away with what had been done and said. However, it was *over*.

We decided we weren't going to appeal. I was tired of living the nightmare every day and having to wonder what was coming next. Oh, well. The entire experience was numbing, but my closeness to Christ was stronger than ever, our family had grown stronger and more unified, and we saw growth and strength in Noah that we could never have imagined. The almost $100,000 that we figured it cost us over that time no longer seemed important. IT WAS OVER! It was a tough two and a half years, but it was time to *truly* move forward.

I needed to find a new life's purpose and area where I could help people and share the Gospel with others. I wanted them to know what they were missing, but more importantly, what they would miss when their earthly bodies run out of time.

There won't be a day in my remaining years I won't think about what happened, but that's collateral damage. I consider it a lesson in growing, and thinking about it that way allows me to remain humble and forgiving. Anybody knows that simply "moving on" is not easy, but baby steps along the way will get you there. Like getting dumped by the Homecoming queen after falling in love with her, it takes time, and you get through little by little each day until it's better.

38

THOSE THAT INFLUENCE YOUR LIFE

W hen we reflect on our lives, recognizing the people who influenced the paths we took to get where we are is crucial. Most of those people are those we look upon and say how great of a person they were, but others may have been influential because they led us down paths of terrible experiences. However, they are all responsible for allowing us to get to the places we are now.

It's a nice ride when things are rosy and fun but complex and challenging when tough times come our way. I don't know of anyone who says, "Oh, boy! I can't wait until adversity hits me. It'll be so much fun!" God has promised us that those times will happen, but He is *always* there to get us through.

> *"'For I know the plans I have for you,' declares the Lord,*
> *'plans to prosper you and not to harm you, plans to give*
> *you hope and a future.'"*

— JEREMIAH 29:11 NIV

You see, there are times that hurt, times when you can't imagine moving forward, and times when you feel all is lost. Not only during my time in Gull Lake did I feel that same way, but other times in almost every stage of my life, too. Being involved in athletics since I can remember undoubtedly provided some of those times.

God allows you to grab Him, and He, in turn, gives you hope and reassurance that He provides. He will fill you with the strength that only He can. Sure, He puts people in your life to help you along your way, but that's part of His plan.

I can't say thank you enough to those that have allowed me to call on the name of the Lord for help and for the experiences I've gone through. I challenge everyone to list ten people—without including family members—who have done that for them. I could certainly name more, but there are ten that come into my mind instantly.

Many of those that I could name helped me remember that things will get better, and the Lord reassured me that was true. And you know what? Things *did* get better.

We are given the promise that life will throw curveballs that seem impossible to hit. He assures us that those tough pitches will make us better hitters as long as we rely on Him for instruction. You might hate trying to hit that curveball, but you become better by practicing. Most people don't necessarily like to practice, but we won't see improvements without it.

> *"Beloved, do not be surprised at the fiery trial when it comes upon you to test you, as though something strange was happening to you. But rejoice insofar as you share Christ's sufferings, that you may also rejoice and be glad when his glory is revealed."*
>
> **— 1 PETER 4:12-13 ESV**

The most important thing I needed to figure out and what everyone reading this needs to remember... I AM NOT THE PERSON OTHERS SAY THAT I AM.

I AM THE PERSON GOD MADE AND THE PERSON HE LOVES.

He will always be with you, even though everyone will, at some point, question who they are.

Just remember, and repeat this out loud if you must: **I AM WHO I AM BY THE GRACE OF GOD.**

39

SWEET HOME ALABAMA

Through my friend Russell, Peg and I found the excitement
of live Bama football from the season tickets we scored on
our second day in Alabama. We didn't even have to go
church shopping. Russell told us about one we might be interested
in, the Church of the Highlands. We went there on our first Sunday
in Tuscaloosa and never visited another church. From the praise and
worship to the messages delivered, it was terrific. Pastor Chris
Hodges was incredibly gifted and funny with several of his sayings
and quips. More about that later.

I continued my Uber driving, made good retirement money, and
talked with a wide range of people. Several opportunities to witness
about God's grace and the gift of salvation came about. When trips
are short, seeing someone turn their lives over to Christ is rare, but
you still hope they'll remember your conversation at some point in
their life.

There was one college student I met while driving that was not a
believer. Peg and I wound up picking him and his girlfriend up for
church a few Sundays, hoping a seed was planted. I may never
know, but I treasure the memory.

Being an Uber driver lent to many exciting rides. I picked up people ranging from Vice Presidents at well-known companies to hookers and everything in between. Everybody got the same welcome, though, and when they asked how I was doing, my answer was the same: "I couldn't be doing any better."

Peg loves the story of when I picked up three girls from a sorority house. They were going on a group date, a weekend trip to New Orleans with a fraternity. These girls had never met the guys they were going with, which I didn't quite understand. The closer they got to their destination, the more nervous they became.

I told them, "Well, girls, I think you've already committed."

One girl said that her date told them that all the other kids were going to a strip bar and that it would be fun. I said, "Girls, if you want me to take you back right now, I'll be happy to do so."

They declined, feeling that they'd better go.

When we pulled up to the three buses taking the kids to New Orleans, those girls were almost in panic attack mode. I got out, helped them with their luggage, and then went up to their dates and introduced myself as one of the girls' fathers. I told the boys to be good to my daughter and her friends, as I'd only shot two people in my life and didn't want any of them to be the third. Those boys weren't laughing at that point, but neither was I. My "daughter's" date did show a new level of respect, so I turned around and told the girls to be safe and said goodbye to the young lady that was supposedly my child. Her response was, "Thanks, Dad. We will."

I left after that, but I sure hope they had a fun and safe weekend in New Orleans.

I also picked up quite a few of the Alabama football players. That was interesting, seeing as how we talked about... Well, football.

One player—I won't mention his name—got in, and I said, "Hey, ____, what are you doing down this way?"

My passengers' names popped up on my phone when I got a call to pick someone up, so I knew in advance who it was, but I decided to have a little fun with him.

He said, "Just getting a workout in."

I asked if it was just for fun or for a class, knowing full well he was an All-American player, who now plays in the NFL. He said it was for football, and I asked if he played for a high school in the area. He grinned and said he played for the university.

My response was, "Well, is your team any good?"

With the absolute most respectful response, he said, "We do what we can do."

I asked if he played at all, and he said that he played a little bit. At that point, I'm sure he was probably thinking, *Who in the world is this idiot not knowing this stuff?*

Finally, I said, "I'm just kidding. I know who you are. We go to all the games and are huge fans."

He shook his head, punched me in the arm, and said he was wondering how in the heck someone lived in Tuscaloosa and didn't know about Alabama football.

Just about any driver probably has some interesting stories to share, especially if they drive at night. I used to drive at night when we lived in Kalamazoo, and it was probably the most entertaining time to drive when people had a few "pops" in them. I stopped when we moved, as Peg and I wanted to be together all of the time.

Even though we enjoyed life in Alabama, we missed two of our kids and our three granddaughters. The MIAAA still wanted me to be involved with the organization, so Peg and I traveled back to Michigan three times a year for meetings, which gave us time to spend time with our family there. It wasn't like seeing them every week, but with FaceTime and our trips, we still saw each other a good bit.

The MIAAA is as good an organization as you can find. When things hit the fan in Gull Lake, those in the leadership area contacted me right away and said they still wanted me in it. Thank goodness. It was nice to have some sort of normalcy in my career continue to be a part of my life.

40

CHURCH OF THE HIGHLANDS

As I mentioned earlier, we decided quickly on attending the
Church of the Highlands for our new worship home. It is
a highly vibrant church with praise and worship music
that rivals any church imaginable, and its the second-largest church
in America, but that includes many different campuses and
correctional facilities throughout the state. In saying that, yes, it is a
nonjudgmental place with the intent of looking to the future and
not worrying about the past in regards to mistakes you may have
made or the things that others may have done to you. Perfect!

As I stated before, when we lived in Michigan, we knew a ton of
people, and people knew who we were. Now we were challenged
with starting over again. Upon our first visit to the church, we didn't
know anyone. Sure, we'd greet others when the pastor instructed us,
but *knowing* people was yet to come. However, once we attended our
first small group a few months later, things changed. It had maybe
fifteen other people, and we found new friends that became a
security blanket for us.

Scott and Lisa Whisenant were the first we became close to and
then others such as Mike and Rebecca Mills, and Chad and
Merideth Green. They took a church the size of ours and turned it

into a much smaller place that gave people a chance to get to know others who had the same love for Christ as we did. The couples mentioned above had several people they were friends with (probably hundreds), as they were involved in the church and the communities of Northport and Tuscaloosa.

It wasn't like we hung out all the time, but we could rely on them for help and support if needed. Saying thank you especially to those three couples does not compare to what we owe them.

Highlands is a church that supports and believes in the Word of God and is also a community full of laughter, outgoing love, and a welcoming atmosphere that's contagious for allowing people to leave the building wanting to share that love with others. If you attend a church and don't laugh, love, get challenged, follow God's Word, and want to share that with others, you may want to find a different church.

Part of our plan for Tuscaloosa was to stay there anywhere from one to four years, and we knew the church and the people would make leaving difficult. However, staying permanently was never our plan. We were hoping to stay until Noah graduated but said that if the right house opened up in the middle of Georgia near Josh and Morgan, we would consider it, and we did, even though we were in the midst of the COVID-19 pandemic.

The pandemic caused issues all over. Fortunately, we lived in a state that didn't close all of its doors. Sure, we wore our masks when we had to, but we still enjoyed life. We went out to eat, celebrated whatever the occasion was with our family, flew on airplanes, drove to Michigan; almost everything we had been doing continued for us.

What was frustrating was the condemnation from some for simply doing ordinary things that we were used to doing. We hunkered down at the beginning of the pandemic, and that was okay for a while. It gave us a chance to watch *Breaking Bad, Ozarks*, and a few other entertainment shows, but once things became more and more known, we felt much more comfortable going out as long as we were safe. However, some couldn't understand or figure out our behavior.

From how we want to feel, criticism, hard times like the

COVID-19 mess, and other sorts of conflict, the proper response is humility. In **PSALM 7**, David dwells on being persecuted but immediately asks God to test his heart and asks Him to reveal things. Then, instead of taking matters into his own hands, he asks the Lord to vindicate him.

It is important to note that we are never to take our own revenge, but rather to leave vengeance to God, as it says in **ROMANS 16**. Then in the New International Version of **ROMANS 12:21**, He tells us,

"Do not be overcome by evil, but overcome evil with good."

In other words, we must leave the situation with God and trust Him to vindicate us in His time and way.

Jesus said we're to bless those who curse us, as in **LUKE 6:28**. Many people use the phrase "kill them with kindness" to explain the simple human process that would go so far in this world if all of us use it. I've finally gotten to the point of asking Him for the grace and humility to examine my own heart and trust Him to be my defender.

Having lived in Michigan for sixty years and moved to the south, people asked how I like it. Honestly, if I knew as a teen what I know now, I'd have moved to the south in a heartbeat once I could be on my own. The weather, overall friendliness of people, and the pace of life are different in a way that suits Peg and me. God delivered us to a much better life down here, but without the previous circumstances that put us through the wringer, it would have probably never happened.

There is so much more living to do, and we are making the most of what we can. Overall, Peg's health has not kept us down, and being blessed is an understatement. Pastor Chris Hodges said something I try to embrace daily: "I have decided that I'm not going to let anything that will ultimately mean nothing keep me from experiencing what ultimately means everything." Amen, and amen.

To this day, it is crazy to think we once lived in Alabama, but I know this to be true... Alabama helped save my life!

41

GEORGIA

I n the early spring of 2020, in the middle of COVID-19, we traveled to Athens, Georgia, to look at real estate. We knew one particular house was probably "the one." It checked off just about every one of our boxes.

So in May, we moved from Tuscaloosa, the city that saved my life, to within ten minutes of Josh and his family. We see them quite often. Morgan's family is also close-knit. Being a member of a country club was not something I would have imagined doing, but here we are. Our new house is perfect for us. One story, on the golf course, and about an hour from our new best friends, Jay and Dawn Carr and their family.

The transition to Georgia from Tuscaloosa was extremely tough. Leaving Tuscaloosa was just as hard as leaving Michigan, and in some ways, even more challenging. It took me a solid month to get out of a funk, and that wasn't a feeling I liked.

Where did I *want* to be? Michigan? Tuscaloosa? I just knew I didn't think Athens, Georgia was it. But then something wonderful happened...

We went to Michigan for a week and a half for MIAAA business and visited Marc and Kelli and their families. When we left, I found myself eager to get back to Athens. Once there, it was like a switch had been flipped! I began loving where I was. I played a lot of golf, exercised regularly, went to the pool, and hung out with Josh's family and the Carrs. Life since then has been exhilarating.

I often think of my stops along the way and the different people I've met. I think about the experiences I went through, as most people probably do, and the tough ones take me back to places I don't want to go. Depression put its grip on me again. Even though I continue to pray that the Lord allows me to move on, after a few years of having continuing depressive episodes, it was suggested I try something proven to help with my diagnosed PTSD. Gotta love modern medicine.

I've said before that I am fortunate that all my kids have great in-laws, but if I didn't talk about our new southern family a bit more, I'd have left out a significant part of our transition into the next stage of our lives.

Something else that's kind of weird, but also sort of funny is that when you grow older, most people start to forget things. For me, I still do pretty darn good but have the occasional lapse of an event, or a name might not jive every once in a while. But I also believe even the sanest people forget something every once in a while. What I can tell you is that whenever a classic Rock and Roll tune comes on, I can remember the words to almost every song. That's good enough for me.

The Miller/Carr/LaFave families have loads of friends, and those friends have turned into our friends. We see them at least once a week, and usually more than that. Yes, they have been blessed financially, but it's what they do with their wealth that's so amazing, and what others in that position should aspire to (I'm sure many do). You would never know that they have what they have, as there are zero times you ever hear them talk that way.

They, and especially their daughter Lucy, have started the Happy Feat organization. Based in Suwanee, Georgia, Happy Feat is a place where people with special needs who are past school age can go and continue on with a sort of school routine. Learning, activities, field trips, and other things are provided to those involved, as well as some great experiences. Over 2,000 people participate in one way or another when they put on their prom. Of course, that's just a glimpse of what they do. Check them out. They can also be found online at happyfeat.org.

Jay Thrasher is a family member with special needs who the Carrs adopted when he was twenty-five years old. He's pretty much the center of attention when he's around, and what a remarkable individual he is! They have taken him from a challenging surrounding and provided him with a normal (wait, seldom is anything "normal" in their house) life, full of love and happiness.

They, especially Josh's wife Morgan, also put on Christmas for the homeless in Athens. Meals, clothing, gifts, and necessities are in colossal abundance, provided to those in that position, and it's done on Christmas Day. Instead of being content to celebrate with their families, they choose to bless others who are not as fortunate. We have participated in the last several years, and feel extremely good about what we see, the number of people giving up their celebrations, and witnessing the joy and happiness of those who come to enjoy Christmas.

Lastly, I've been able to bear witness to a relationship that's not only unique but an example of the kind of people we're dealing with now. There's a man, Frankie, who has been working with the Carrs for many years. He is gifted in dealing with electricity and does a lot of work in the neighborhood.

The area in which Carrs live has several current and former Atlanta Braves and Falcons players. Frankie, who is from Mexico, has done work for many of them. In one case, he did a job for a professional baseball player who told him, "No, you earned more than that!" after Frankie gave him the cost. Frankie turned down the additional money.

The man showed Frankie a bed with rails made out of baseball bats that some well-known players had signed. Tom Glavine, Sammy Sosa, Mark McGuire, and Chipper Jones, to name just a few. This bed was unique, and he wanted to give it to Frankie. But Frankie said no, it was too much, and that he already had received his compensation.

Two things: the ballplayer was someone who appreciated Frankie's skill and wanted Frankie to be able to have a good life in America and feel valued; and also, Frankie was honest enough to say he'd already been paid and turned down an additional offer he felt he hadn't yet earned.

My friends, these are the immigrants we should be carefully welcoming with open arms from Mexico.

The relationship that Frankie and Jay have is remarkable. They are both men trying to be good people, who work hard for their families. Frankie understands how fortunate he is to be in America, and Jay wants to help people like Frankie in the worst way. They are close friends who see each other almost daily. Frankie is more than just someone who tackles the most complex electrical jobs and builds things to the specifications most builders envy. He's also formed a friendship with someone who wants to give help and support to so many. If something needs to get done, Jay and Frankie are there together to accomplish it.

Jay has turned into my "partner in crime," and we've become very close. It's been my pleasure.

Yes, they are now part of our family, and we are a part of theirs. They have not been given anything and have gone through things in life that have been more challenging than I would ever want to go through. Dawn can take on four major tasks and complete them all perfectly while running a business she started from scratch. Jay works his tail off, and he is a great friend who made my transfer to Athens a wonderful thing.

It's impossible to say how grateful we are for them and what they've done for our entire family. When they visit Josh and Morgan, we go also, and that almost always includes dinner somewhere. That makes us a lucky three-for-three in having great in-laws. One more to go, but we're hopeful the run doesn't stop. Based on our view of things now, it won't.

As we settle into our new season of life, we are lucky to live so close to Josh. Therefore, we get to babysit our granddaughter, Stevie Lu, about four days a week. Being retired and babysitting? We wouldn't want it any other way. When we lived in Michigan, we had three granddaughters within fifteen minutes of us but couldn't spend as much time with them as we do now because we worked so much.

Besides golf, exercise, babysitting, and doing family events, we sure don't have much free time. It's mostly all fun and games, but you never know what pitch He's going to throw next. Never prepared for it, don't want it, and despise going through it. Yep, the hard part of life is… Well, it's hard! The good news? I know where I'm going when I die because God has promised me that.

There is one of two ways you'll spend eternity once you go, and I'm pretty sure nobody wants to go the downward route. You don't need to be perfect—I'm living proof of that—and there are not enough good deeds in the world that you can do to buy your way into Heaven. Salvation, you accepting Christ as your Savior, is the *only* way. Please choose wisely.

If you're unsure about where you'll be for eternity, say something like, "Lord, thank You for loving me unconditionally, despite my shortcomings. I ask You to forgive all my sins, and I am so thankful that Jesus was sent here by You to die on the cross to forgive me of all sins, past, present, and future. I also acknowledge that He is the ruler of all, and I will follow Him forever."

That's pretty simple, but it's the path to Heaven. If you say it and believe in your heart that Jesus is Lord, I'll see you in Heaven.

Remember when I said that February 25th, 2015 was the worst day of my life?

Well, it was the beginning of a phase of recovery, forgiveness, an entirely new life. As it turns out, it may have been one of the best days of my life. Almost every day is fun again, and the lessons I've learned during those tough times have been instrumental in leading me to this great life I have now.

AFTERWORD

I've gone from walking to Fred's Market and watching some crazy horse race on Saturday nights to somewhere in the fourth quarter of my life, but there is no guarantee when "that day" will pop up. So, in this part of the game, I want to do fun things, spend as much time with my family in the north and south as I can, see a friend once in a while, and experience many more of the great aspects that are out there.

For decades, my life has been incredibly blessed. Through good times and bad, I've learned that if you're worried about what people say about you, it can hurt and damage the "self."

Some may say, "I don't care how people feel about me," but true self-reflection shows we'd all rather have people say nice things about us rather than bad. For some, hurtful words bother us less, but all of us have the thought that we'd rather have others respect and like what we've said and done, what we represent, and what type of person we are.

The good news? We have a way to allow that "self" to be a lot less offensive than what some might feel. Why? The Lord has given us a way, even though we, as humans, may never feel free.

Amazingly, I didn't die. Why didn't I die when I fell out of that tree as a kid? Why didn't I die when I drove my car like a madman, or when Brian and I drove motorcycles at eighty miles per hour after drinking, or when all of those other situations occurred? God has more plans for my life. *That's* why!

Why would anyone want to be thought of as no longer helpful? He is leading you toward great things, no matter how old or young you are. Remember that salvation prayer? Let Him lead you in a direction where you'll have many more experiences, but realize that there is always an explanation. It's just that we don't know what the answer is… yet!

> *"Jesus and his disciples went on to the villages around*
> *Caesarea Philippi. On the way, He asked them, 'Who do*
> *people say I am?'"*
>
> **— MARK 8:27 NIV**

If you think for a minute that He didn't know what people said about him or believed they didn't know who he was, be it good or bad, try to understand Him more. He wanted his disciples to realize that there is a way to not worry about what others feel about you or say who or what you are.

No matter what you have done or what you have said, Jesus loves you unconditionally. Try to imagine that. If you've done something wrong, Jesus loves you unconditionally. If you've said something wrong, Jesus loves you unconditionally. You are who He has created, and He loves you for that.

You can repent at any time in your life and have all the sins you've committed forgiven. He'll give you a fresh start. I have decided to follow Jesus, and although I am still a sinner, He will forgive me.

If you've decided to have Him as your savior, trust that when you die—and I'll lay odds on it that you *will* die—all of those bad things won't be remembered. However, He will look at all the good you've done and reward you accordingly. But you've got to get there first. You'll still get into Heaven if you've accepted Him, but it's the promised rewards you'll receive that will make it amazing when you get there. Please don't ask me to tell you exactly what they are because I haven't been there. *YET!*

From my time growing up in Romeo, Michigan, to Kalamazoo, Michigan, to Tuscaloosa, Alabama, to Athens, Georgia, my life has been filled with more blessings and happiness than I deserve. If you haven't accepted Jesus as your Lord and Savior by now, join the party that awaits you. It'll be a decision that you'll be more than happy with for eternity, and that, my friends, is a long time.

Praise the Lord from whom all blessings flow!

ACKNOWLEDGMENTS

As a first-time author, you ask yourself many times, "Why am I doing this?" However, I started this project at the urging of my daughter, Kelli, and I want to acknowledge her for the suggestion and encouragement. I'm not sure she anticipated I would complete this, but it was something I so needed to do.

Without the help of my editor, Jody Freeman, I could not have completed the final project and been able to maneuver through the specifics of writing the dream I've had. Her participation has been beyond important and appreciated, and I am eager to work with her again on other books I'm writing.